Study Guide

Macroeconomics

NINTH EDITION

Roger A. Arnold
California State University, San Marcos

SOUTH-WESTERN
CENGAGE Learning

Australia • Brazil • Japan • Korea • Mexico • Singapore • Spain • United Kingdom • United States

SOUTH-WESTERN
CENGAGE Learning

**Macroeconomics, 9E
Study Guide**

Roger A. Arnold

Vice President of Editorial, Business: Jack W. Calhoun

Vice President/Editor-in-Chief: Alex von Rosenberg

Senior Acquisitions Editor: Michael W. Worls

Senior Developmental Editors: Jennifer E. Thomas, Laura Bofinger

Editorial Assistant: Lena Mortis

Marketing Manager: John Carey

Marketing Communications Manager: Sarah Greber

Senior Content Project Manager: Kim Kusnerak

Media Editor: Deepak Kumar

Senior Manufacturing Buyer: Sandee Milewski

Compositor: PrePress

Senior Art Director: Michelle Kunkler

Cover Designer: Ke Design/Mason, Ohio

Cover Image: © Digital Vision Photography

Rights Account Manager—Text: Mollika Basu

For product information and technology assistance, contact us at
**Cengage Learning Customer & Sales Support,
1-800-354-9706**

For permission to use material from this text or product, submit all requests online at **www.cengage.com/permissions**
Further permissions questions can be emailed to
permissionrequest@cengage.com

ISBN-13: 978-0-324-78553-1
ISBN-10: 0-324-78553-4

South-Western Cengage Learning
5191 Natorp Boulevard
Mason, OH 45040
USA

Cengage Learning products are represented in Canada by Nelson Education, Ltd.

For your course and learning solutions, visit www.cengage.com
Purchase any of our products at your local college store or at our preferred online store **www.ichapters.com**

Printed in Canada
1 2 3 4 5 6 7 12 11 10 09

Contents

Chapter 1
What Economics Is About

What This Chapter Is About
This chapter is an introduction to economics. Economics is defined and a few of the important concepts in economics are discussed – such as scarcity, opportunity cost, and more. Also, this chapter introduces you to the economic way of thinking.

Key Concepts in the Chapter
    a.   good
    b.   bad
    c.   scarcity
    d.   opportunity cost
    e.   decisions made at the margin
    f.   efficiency
    g.   exchange or trade
    h.   positive and normative economics

- A **good** is anything that gives a person utility or satisfaction.
- A **bad** is anything that gives a person disutility or dissatisfaction.
- **Scarcity** is the condition under which people's wants (for goods) are greater than the resources available to satisfy those wants.
- **Opportunity cost** is the most highly valued opportunity or alternative forfeited when a choice is made.
- When we make **decisions at the margin**, we compare the marginal benefits and marginal costs of things.
- Efficiency exists when the marginal benefits of doing something equal the marginal costs of doing that something.
- **Exchange** or **trade** is the process of giving up one thing for something else.
- **Positive economics** deals with "what is," and **normative economics** deals with what someone thinks "should be."

Review Questions

1.   Is scarcity the condition under which people have infinite wants?

2.   What is the difference between a *good* and a *bad*?

3.   Give an example of when something is a good one day, and a bad some other day?

4.   What is the opportunity cost of your reading this study guide?

5.   If the opportunity cost of smoking cigarettes rises, fewer people will smoke. Why?

6.   What is a synonym (in economics) for the word *additional*?

7.   If Harriet is thinking of studying for one more hour, she considers the marginal benefits and marginal costs of studying for one more hour—not the total benefits and total costs. Why does she consider marginal benefits and costs and not total benefits and costs?

8.   In the text the author discussed the unintended effects of wearing seatbelts. Come up with an example of an unintended effect of something.

9.   What is the relationship between scarcity and choice? Between scarcity and opportunity cost?

10.   What is the relationship between thinking in terms of "what would have been" and opportunity cost?

11.   Is it possible to study too much? Explain your answer.

12.   What are the four categories of resources?

13.   Why do people enter into exchanges or trades?

14.   Why do people want fewer bads and more goods?

15.   What does it mean if someone has exercised enough to receive all the net benefits from exercising?

16.   Find an economic concept in the following scenario: Jim is at the fast food restaurant paying for his
        order.

17.   What does it mean to say there is no free lunch?

18.   What does it mean to say there are no $10 bills on the sidewalk?

19.   What is the difference between microeconomics and macroeconomics?

20.   What is the difference between positive and normative economics?

Problems

1.   Draw a flow chart that shows the relationship between scarcity, choice, and opportunity cost.

2. Jim is considering going to college. He knows there are benefits and costs to attending college. In the table below you will see various factors identified in the first column. Determine whether the factor relates to the cost of going to college or to the benefit of going to college. Next, identify whether the specified change in the factor raises or lowers the cost or benefit of going to college. If it raises the benefit of going to college, place an upward arrow (↑) in the benefits column; if it lowers the benefit of going to college, place a downward arrow (↓) in the benefits column. Do the same for the costs column. Finally, identify whether the change in the factor makes it more likely (Yes or No) Jim will go to college.

Factor	Benefits of attending college	Costs of attending college	More likely to go to college? Yes or No
Jim thought he would earn $20 an hour if he didn't go to college, but learns that he will earn $35 an hour instead.			
His friends are going to college and he likes being around his friends.			
The salary gap between college graduates and high school graduates has widened.			
Jim learns something about himself: he doesn't like to study.			
The college he is thinking about attending just opened a satellite campus near Jim's home.			
The economy has taken a downturn and it looks like there are very few jobs for high school graduates right now.			

3. Identify each of the following questions as related to either a microeconomic or macroeconomic topic.

    a. Why did that firm charge a higher price?

    b. When will the economy slow down?

    c. When will the unemployment rate fall?

    d. Are interest rates rising?

    e. How does that firm decide how many cars it will produce this year?

    f. What is the price of a really fast computer?

    g. Why did that restaurant go out of business?

4. There is an opportunity cost to everything you do. In the first column you will see an activity
    identified. In the second column, identify what you think the opportunity cost (for you) would be if
    you undertook that particular activity.

Activity	Opportunity Cost
Study one more hour each night	
Take a trip to someplace you have always wanted to visit	
Sit in the back of the room in one of your classes	
Talk up more in class	
Get a regular medical checkup	
Surf the Web more	

What Is Wrong?
In each of the statements below, something is wrong. Identify what is wrong in the space provided.

1. People have finite wants and infinite resources.

2. People prefer more bads to fewer bads.

3. Scarcity is an effect of competition.

4. The lower the opportunity cost of playing tennis, the less likely a person will play tennis.

5. Microeconomics is the branch of economics that deals with human behavior and choices as they
    relate to highly aggregate markets or the entire economy.

6. Positive economics is to normative economics as opinion is to truth.

7. Because there are rationing devices, there will always be scarcity.

8.   The four factors of production, or resources, are land, labor, capital, and profit.

9.   In a two-person exchange, one person is made better off while the other person is made worse off.

10.   If X is a good for Smith, it must then be a good for Jones too.

Multiple Choice
Circle the correct answer.

1.   Economics is the science of
      a.   human relationships in an economic setting.
      b.   business and prices.
      c.   scarcity.
      d.   goods and services.

2.   Scarcity exists
      a.   in only poor countries of the world.
      b.   in all countries of the world.
      c.   only when society does not employ all its resources in an efficient way.
      d.   only when society produces too many frivolous or silly goods.

3.   Which of the following statements is true?
      a.   Both a millionaire and a poor person must deal with scarcity.
      b.   People would have to make choices even if scarcity did not exist.
      c.   Scarcity is a relatively new problem in the world's history; it has not always existed.
      d.   It is likely that one day scarcity will no longer exist.

4.   Which of the following statements is true?
      a.   Coca-Cola is a good for everyone, even someone who has an allergy to Coca-Cola.
      b.   If you pay someone to take X off your hands, then it is likely that X is a bad.
      c.   It is possible, but not likely, that someone can obtain both utility and disutility from a bad.
      d.   If there is more of good A than people want at zero price, then good A is an economic good.

5.   Kristin Taylor had a safety inspection performed on her car last week and it passed with flying colors.
      How is this likely to affect her future driving behavior, compared to a situation in which cars did not
      get safety inspections at all?
      a.   She will probably drive faster, and the probability of having an accident is reduced.
      b.   She will probably drive slower, and the probability of having an accident is reduced.
      c.   She will probably drive faster, and the probability of having an accident is increased.
      d.   She will probably drive slower, and the probability of having an accident is increased.

6.   Frank is 19 years old and is an actor in a soap opera, "One Life to Ruin." He earns $100,000 a year.
      Cassandra is also 19 years old and works in a local clothing store. She earns $9 an hour. Which of the
      two persons is more likely to attend college and for what reason?
      a.   Cassandra, because she is smarter.
      b.   Frank, because he has higher opportunity costs of attending college than Cassandra.
      c.   Cassandra, because she has lower opportunity costs of attending college than Frank.
      d.   Frank, because he earns a higher income than Cassandra.

7. Which of the following is an example of a *positive* statement?
    a. If you drop a quarter off the top of the Sears building in Chicago, it will fall to the ground.
    b. The minimum wage should be raised to eight dollars an hour.
    c. There is too much crime in the United States; something should be done about it.
    d. People should learn to get along with each other.

8. Which of the following topics is a microeconomics topic?
    a. the study of what influences the nation's unemployment rate
    b. the study of how changes in the nation's money supply affect the nation's output
    c. the study of prices in the automobile market
    d. the study of what affects the inflation rate

9. "Productive resources" include which of the following?
    a. land, labor, money, management
    b. land, labor, money, entrepreneurship
    c. land, labor, capital, entrepreneurship
    d. land, labor, natural resources, entrepreneurship

10. Efficiency exists if
    a. marginal benefits are greater than marginal costs.
    b. marginal costs are greater than marginal benefits.
    c. marginal costs equal zero.
    d. marginal costs equal marginal benefits.
    e. none of the above

True-False
Write a "T" or "F" after each statement.

11. A good is anything from which individuals receive utility. _____

12. If there is no explicit charge for a good, it is not a scarce good. _____

13. Scarcity implies that choices will be made. _____

14. The higher a person's opportunity cost of time, the more likely a person will stand in a long line to buy a ticket to a concert or some other event, *ceteris paribus*. _____

15. As economists use the term, a "good" is a tangible item that you can see and touch (rather than an intangible service). _____

Fill in the Blank
Write the correct word in the blank.

16. _____ is the branch of economics that deals with highly aggregated markets or the entire economy.

17. One more unit of something is the _____ unit.

18. A good that is used to produce other goods, yet is not a natural resource, is called a _____ good.

19. The person who organizes production in a firm and is responsible for recognizing new business opportunities is an _____.

20. _____ is the process of giving up one thing for something else.

Chapter 2
Economic Activities: Producing and Trading

What This Chapter Is About
People do it everyday—produce goods and enter into trades. They might produce a desk, computer, or book. They might trade $10 for a book or $2 for a loaf of bread. This chapter is about both producing and trading.

Key Concepts in the Chapter
  a.   exchange
  b.   terms of exchange
  c.   transaction costs
  d.   comparative advantage
  e.   production possibilities frontier
  f.   efficiency
  g.   inefficiency

- **Exchange** is the process of trading one thing for another.
- The **terms of exchange** refer to how much of one thing is traded for how much of something else. For example, the terms of exchange may be $2,000 for one computer.
- **Transaction costs** are the costs associated with the time and effort needed to search out, negotiate, and consummate an exchange.
- **Comparative advantage** refers to the situation in which someone can produce a good at lower opportunity cost than someone else. For example, if Jones can produce good Z at lower cost than Smith, then Jones has a comparative advantage in the production of good Z.
- A **production possibilities frontier (PPF)** represents the possible combination of two goods that an economy can produce in a certain period of time, under the conditions of a given state of technology, no unemployed resources, and efficient production.
- **Efficiency** implies the impossibility of gains in one area without losses in another.
- **Inefficiency** implies the possibility of gains in one area without losses in another.

Review Questions

1.   José is thinking of buying a house. Is he in the *ex ante* or *ex post* position with respect to exchange?

2.   How is economic growth represented in the production possibilities frontier framework?

3. How are choice and opportunity cost represented in the production possibilities frontier framework?

4. Consumers prefer terms of exchange in their favor. What does this mean?

5. Are the transaction costs of buying a hamburger at a fast food restaurant higher or lower than the transaction costs of selling a house? Explain your answer.

6. Give an example of an exchange with a third-party negative effect.

7. Janet can produce either (a) 10 units of X and 20 units of Y, or (b) 20 units of X and 5 units of Y. What is the cost (to Janet) of producing one unit of X? One unit of Y?

8. Why does specialization and trade benefit people?

9. Why do people trade? What is the necessary condition for trade to take place?

10. Give an example that illustrates the law of increasing costs.

11. What does a straight-line production possibilities frontier (PPF) indicate about costs?

12. What does a bowed-outward (concave downward) PPF indicate about costs?

13. A country can be at either point A or B on its PPF. What does this fact have to do with the economic concept of *tradeoff*?

14. Identify two things that can shift a PPF outward (to the right).

    a.

    b.

15. Give an example of an advance in technology.

16. How does profit motivate action?

Problems

1. Vernon bought a hat for $40. Identify more favorable terms of exchange for Vernon.

2. Karen's maximum buying price is $400 for good X. Randy's minimum selling price is $350 for good X. Currently, Karen and Randy have to each pay $60 in transaction costs to buy and sell good X. If an entrepreneur charges both the buyer and the seller $5, what is the minimum reduction in transaction costs that that entrepreneur must bring about (for each person) before the trade will be actualized at a price of $370?

3. Can you draw a PPF for grades? Use the data (that follow) to draw a production possibilities frontier for grades.

Hours spent studying Sociology	Grade in Sociology	Hours spent studying Economics	Grade in Economics
6	90	0	60
5	85	1	65
4	80	2	70
3	75	3	75
2	70	4	80
1	65	5	85
0	60	6	90

Grade in
Sociology

Grade in Economics

4. Using the data in the previous question, what is the opportunity cost of earning a 65 instead of a 60 in Economics?

5. Identify the points on the PPF that are efficient.

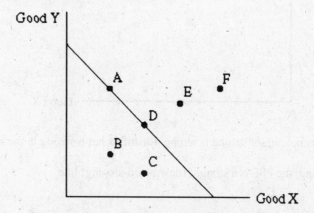

6. Which points on the PPF (in the previous question) are inefficient?

7. Which points on the PPF (in question 5) are unattainable?

8. Suppose that point C, with 100 units of good X and 200 units of good Y, is an efficient point. Could point D, with 75 units of good X and 250 units of good Y, also be an efficient point? Explain your answer.

9. Within a PPF framework, diagrammatically represent the effect of a war that destroys people and property.

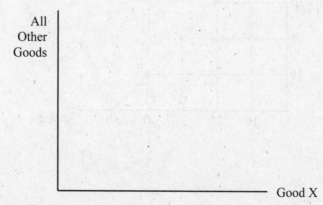

10. Within a PPF framework, diagrammatically represent the effect of an advance in technology.

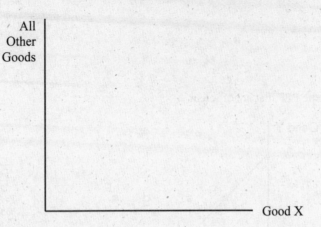

What Is Wrong?
In each of the statements below, something is wrong. Identify what is wrong in the space provided.

1. If costs are increasing, the PPF is a straight (downward-sloping) line.

2. If Jones can produce either (a) 100 units of X and 100 units of Y or (b) 200 units of X and zero units of Y, then he has a comparative advantage in the production of Y.

3. The following PPF represents a two-for-one opportunity cost of apples.

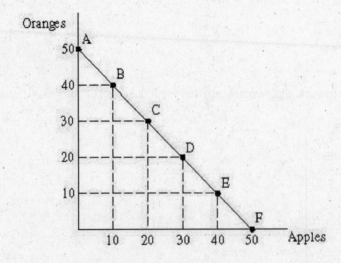

4.   There are probably more unemployed resources at point A than at point D.

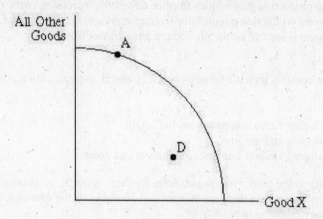

5.   Efficiency implies the possibility of gains in one area without losses in another area.

6.   If Georgina reads one more book, she will have to give up doing something else. This shows that Georgina is inefficient.

7.   If Bobby can produce either (a) 100 units of good X and 50 units of good Y, or (b) 25 units of good X and 80 units of good Y, then the cost of 1 unit of good X is 1.5 units of good Y.

8.   John says, "I bought this sweater yesterday and I think I got a bad deal." It follows that in the *ex ante* position John thought he would be better off with the sweater than with the money he paid for it, but in the *ex post* position he prefers the money to the sweater.

Multiple Choice
Circle the correct answer.

1.   Which of the following statements is true?
     a.   The production possibilities frontier is always bowed outward.
     b.   The production possibilities frontier is usually bowed outward.
     c.   The production possibilities frontier is never bowed outward.
     d.   The production possibilities frontier is usually a straight line.

2. Which of the following statements is false?
    a. A straight-line production possibilities frontier represents increasing costs.
    b. A bowed outward production possibilities frontier represents constant costs.
    c. An efficient point is located on the production possibilities frontier.
    d. a and b

3. If there is always a constant tradeoff between goods A and B, the production possibilities frontier between A and B is
    a. circular.
    b. a downward-sloping curve bowed toward the origin.
    c. a downward-sloping straight line.
    d. a downward-sloping straight line that is broken at one point.

4. Consider two points on the production possibilities frontier: point X, at which there are 100 cars and 78 trucks, and point Y, at which there are 90 cars and 70 trucks. If the economy is currently at point X, the opportunity cost of moving to point Y is
    a. 12 cars.
    b. 1 truck.
    c. 10 cars.
    d. 79 trucks.
    e. none of the above

5. If it is possible to increase production of one good without getting less of another, then currently the economy is
    a. operating efficiently.
    b. sluggish.
    c. operating inefficiently.
    d. operating at technological inferiority.

6. The production possibilities frontier represents the possible combinations of two goods that an economy can produce
    a. in a certain time.
    b. in a certain time, under the condition of a given state of resources.
    c. given that there are not unemployed resources.
    d. under the condition of efficient production.
    e. None of the answers is complete enough.

7. When the economy exhibits inefficiency, it is not producing the
    a. maximum output with the available resources and technology.
    b. minimum output with minimum resources and technology.
    c. the goods and services consumers wish to buy.
    d. b and c

8. When Beverly trades $60 for good X, economists assume that she is trading something
    a. of less value to her for something of more value to her.
    b. of more value to her for something of less value to her.
    c. that gives her less utility for something that gives her more utility.
    d. a and c
    e. none of the above

9. The _____ refer(s) to how much of one thing is traded for how much of something else.
    a. exchange process
    b. terms of exchange
    c. duality prices
    d. non-monetary pricing process
    e. double pricing process

10. Transaction costs are
    a. the costs associated with the time and effort needed to search out, negotiate, and consummate an exchange.
    b. the costs a consumer pays in the *ex ante* position.
    c. the costs a seller pays in the *ex post* position.
    d. identical to the terms of exchange.
    e. always higher for buyers than sellers.

11. If Mark and Bob are not currently trading $10 for a book, it may be because
    a. transaction costs are too high.
    b. transaction costs are too low.
    c. at least one of the two individuals does not think he would be made better off by the trade.
    d. both individuals think they will be made worse off by the trade.
    e. a, c, and d

12. If Sean can bake bread at a lower cost than Jason, and Jason can produce paintings at a lower cost then Sean, it follows that
    a. Sean has a comparative advantage in paintings and Jason has a comparative advantage in baking bread.
    b. Both Sean and Jason have a comparative advantage in baking bread.
    c. Both Sean and Jason have a comparative advantage in producing paintings.
    c. Sean has a comparative advantage in baking bread and Jason has a comparative advantage in producing paintings.
    d. There is not enough information to answer the question.

13. Vernon can produce the following combinations of X and Y: 100X and 20Y, 50X and 30Y, or 0X or 40Y. The opportunity cost of one unit of Y for Vernon is
    a. five units of Y.
    b. two units of Y.
    c. three units of Y.
    d. one-half unit of Y.
    e. none of the above

True-False
Write a "T" or "F" after each statement.

14. Because scarcity exists, individuals and societies must make choices. ____

15. If the production of good X comes in terms of increasing costs of good Y, then the production possibilities frontier between the two goods is a downward-sloping straight line. ____

16. Economic growth shifts the production possibilities frontier inward. ____

17. Productive efficiency is diagrammatically represented as a point on the production possibilities frontier. ____

18. Without scarcity, there would be no production possibilities frontier. ____

Fill in the Blank
Write the correct word in the blank.

19. _____ implies it is possible to obtain gains in one area without losses in another.

20. _____ implies it is impossible to obtain gains in one area without losses in another.

21. At point A on a production possibilities frontier there are 50 apples and 60 oranges. At point B there are 49 apples and 68 oranges. If the economy is currently at point B, the opportunity cost of moving to point A is _____ oranges.

22. The higher the _____ _____ of making an exchange, the less likely the exchange will be made.

23. The higher the _____ _____ of doing X, the less likely X will be done.

24. A point on a PPF is considered to represent a combination of two goods that is _____.

25. A _____ _____ PPF represents constant costs.

Chapter 3
Supply and Demand: Theory

What This Chapter Is About

This chapter is about markets. A market has two sides—a demand side and a supply side. The chapter first discusses demand, then supply, then it puts both sides of the market together and discusses the price and quantity of goods.

Key Concepts in the Chapter

- a. demand
- b. law of demand
- c. supply
- d. law of supply
- e. equilibrium price
- f. shortage
- g. surplus
- h. consumers' surplus
- i. producers' surplus

- **Demand** is the willingness and ability to buy different quantities of a good at different prices over some period of time. Keep in mind that if a person doesn't have both the willingness and ability to buy a good, then there is no demand.
- The **law of demand** states that price and quantity demanded are inversely related, *ceteris paribus*. This means that as price rises, quantity demanded falls, and as price falls, quantity demanded rises, *ceteris paribus*.
- **Supply** is the willingness and ability to produce and offer to sell different quantities of a good at different prices over some period of time.
- The **law of supply** states that price and quantity supplied are directly related, *ceteris paribus*. This means that as price rises, quantity supplied rises, and as price falls, quantity supplied falls, *ceteris paribus*.
- **Equilibrium price** is the price at which the quantity demanded of a good equals the quantity supplied. For example, if, at $40, the quantity supplied of good X is 100 units, and quantity demanded of good X is also 100 units, then $40 is the equilibrium price.
- **Equilibrium quantity** is the quantity that corresponds to equilibrium price. At equilibrium, quantity demanded = quantity supplied = equilibrium quantity.
- A **shortage** exists in a market if quantity demanded is greater than quantity supplied. If buyers want to buy 100 units of good X, and sellers only want to sell 30 units, then there is a shortage.
- A **surplus** exists in a market if quantity supplied is greater than quantity demanded. If buyers want to buy 100 units of good X, and sellers want to sell 300 units, then there is a surplus.
- **Consumers' surplus** is the difference between the maximum buying price and price paid. For example, if Smith is willing to pay a maximum of $40 for good X, and he only has to pay $10, then the difference, or $30, is consumers' surplus.
- **Producers' surplus** is the difference between the price paid and the minimum selling price. For example, if Jones is willing to sell good X for $10, but is paid $50, then the difference, or $40, is producers' surplus.

Review Questions

1. What does the law of demand state?

2. What does it mean to say that price and quantity demanded are inversely related?

3. What is quantity demanded?

4. How does quantity demanded differ from demand?

5. Demand is a function of five factors. Stated differently, if there is a change in any of these five factors, demand will either increase or decrease. What are these five factors?

    a.

    b.

    c.

    d.

    e.

6. If demand for a good increases, will the demand curve (that represents the good) shift to the right or to the left?

7. If demand for a good decreases, will the demand curve (that represents the good) shift to the right or to the left?

8. What is quantity supplied?

9. If a supply curve is vertical, what does this mean?

10. If a supply curve is upward-sloping, what does this mean?

11. Supply is a function of six factors. Stated differently, if there is a change in any of these six factors, supply will either increase or decrease. What are these six factors?

      a.

      b.

      c.

      d.

      e.

      f.

12. If the supply of a good increases, will the supply curve (that represents the good) shift to the right or to the left?

13. If the supply of a good decreases, will the supply curve (that represents the good) shift to the right or to the left?

14. Consider the standard supply and demand diagram. The demand curve is downward-sloping and the supply curve is upward-sloping.

    What is on the horizontal axis?

    What is on the vertical axis?

15. What is the difference between the relative price of a good and the absolute price of a good?

16. Demand rises and supply is constant. What happens to equilibrium price and quantity?

17. Supply rises and demand is constant. What happens to equilibrium price and quantity?

18. Demand rises by more than supply rises. What happens to equilibrium price and quantity?

19. Supply falls by more than demand rises. What happens to equilibrium price and quantity?

20. If price rises, what happens to consumers' surplus?

Problems

1. There are many factors that can directly affect supply and demand and indirectly affect price and quantity. In the first column we identify a change in a given factor. How does the change in the factor affect supply or demand? How does it affect price and quantity? Draw an upward arrow (↑) in the demand column if demand rises and a downward arrow (↓) if demand falls. The same holds for supply, equilibrium price, and equilibrium quantity.

Factor	Demand	Supply	Equilibrium Price	Equilibrium Quantity
Price of a substitute rises				
Price of a complement falls				
Income rises (normal good)				
Income falls (inferior good)				
Price of relevant resource rises				
Technology advances				
Quota				
Number of buyers rises				
Number of sellers rises				
Buyers expect higher price				
Sellers expect higher price				
Tax on production				
Preferences become more favorable with respect to the good				

2. Draw a rise in demand that is greater than a rise in supply.

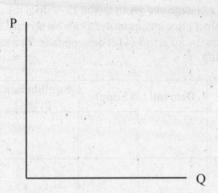

3. Draw a fall in supply that is greater than an increase in demand.

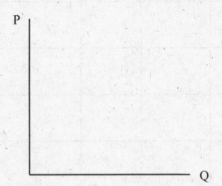

4. What area(s) does consumers' surplus equal at 100 units?

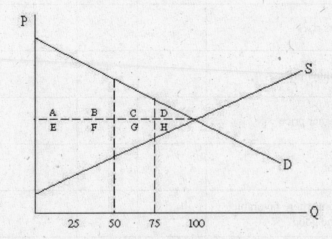

5.   What area(s) does producers' surplus equal at equilibrium quantity?

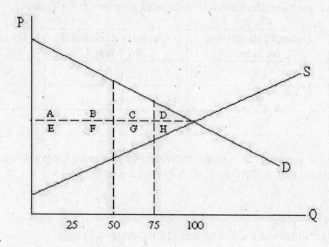

6.   What is the shortage equal to at a price ceiling of $6?

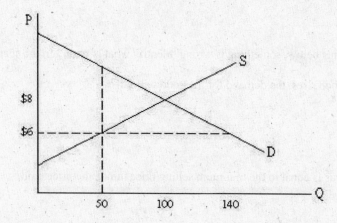

7.   What is the surplus equal to at a price floor of $10?

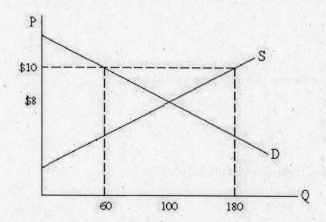

8. There are two buyers in a market, John and Mary. Below you see the quantity demanded for each at various prices. What is the quantity demanded (on the market demand curve) at each price specified? Write in the various quantities demanded in the spaces provided in the table.

Price	Quantity demanded by John	Quantity demanded by Mary	Quantity demanded (market demand)
$10	100	130	
$12	80	120	
$14	50	100	

9. If the price ceiling for good X is $4, and the maximum buying price for good X is $10, what is the highest price for a good that is "tied" to good X (as in a tie-in sale)?

10. Give an example that illustrates the law of diminishing marginal utility.

What Is Wrong?
In each of the statements below, something is wrong. Identify what is wrong in the space provided.

1. If the price of a good rises, the demand for the good will fall.

2. Consumers' surplus is equal to the minimum selling price minus the price paid.

3. As income rises, demand for a normal good rises; as income falls, demand for an inferior good falls.

4. The supply curve for Picasso paintings is upward-sloping.

5. As price rises, supply rises; as price falls, supply falls.

6. Quantity demanded is greater than supply when there is a shortage.

7. If supply rises, and demand is constant, equilibrium price rises and equilibrium quantity rises.

8. The law of diminishing marginal utility states that as a consumer consumes additional units of a good, each successive unit gives him or her more utility than the previous unit.

9. According to the law of demand, as the price of a good rises, the quantity demanded of the good rises, *ceteris paribus*.

Multiple Choice
Circle the correct answer.

1. The law of demand states that
    a. price and demand are inversely related, *ceteris paribus*.
    b. price and demand are directly related, *ceteris paribus*.
    c. price and quantity demanded are directly related, *ceteris paribus*.
    d. price and quantity demanded are inversely related, *ceteris paribus*.

2. Which of the following persons would be most likely to prefer first-come-first-served (FCFS) as a rationing device?
    a. A person who has just returned from visiting a busy city.
    b. A person who has just returned from visiting a small town.
    c. A person with low opportunity cost of time.
    d. A person with high opportunity cost of time.

3. At a price ceiling (below equilibrium price),
    a. there is a surplus.
    b. quantity supplied is greater than quantity demanded.
    c. quantity demanded equals quantity supplied.
    d. supply equals demand.
    e. quantity demanded is greater than quantity supplied.

4. Which of the following statements is true?
    a. A demand schedule is the same thing as a demand curve.
    b. A downward-sloping demand curve is the graphical representation of the law of demand.
    c. Quantity demanded is a relationship between price and demand.
    d. Quantity demanded is the same as demand.

5. Because of a price ceiling on light bulbs, the quantity demanded of light bulbs exceeds the quantity supplied. The owner of the light bulbs decided to sell them on a first-come-first-served basis. This is an example of a
   a. surplus.
   b. tie-in sale.
   c. nonprice rationing device.
   d. black market.
   e. none of the above

6. A neutral good is a good
   a. the demand for which does not change as income falls.
   b. the demand for which does not change as income rises.
   c. the demand for which rises as income falls.
   d. the demand for which falls as income rises.
   e. a and b

7. If the absolute price of good X is $600 and the absolute price of good Y is $400, then the relative price of good Y is
   a. 2 units of X.
   b. 2/3 unit of X.
   c. 1-1/3 unit of X.
   d. 1-1/2 unit of X.
   e. none of the above

8. If an increase in income leads to an increase in the demand for sausage, then sausage is
   a. an essential good.
   b. a normal good.
   c. a luxury good.
   d. a discretionary good.

9. Which of the following can shift the demand curve rightward?
   a. an increase in income
   b. an increase in the price of a substitute good
   c. an increase in the price of a complementary good
   d. all of the above
   e. a and b

10. Which of the following cannot increase the demand for good X?
    a. an increase in income
    b. a decrease in the price of good X
    c. an increase in the price of a substitute good
    d. more buyers
    e. a change in preferences in favor of good X

11. The law of supply states that price and quantity supplied are
    a. directly related.
    b. inversely related.
    c. inversely related, *ceteris paribus*.
    d. directly related, *ceteris paribus*.

12. A change in the quantity supplied of a good is directly brought about by a
    a. change in the good's own price.
    b. decrease in income.
    c. technological advance.
    d. fall in the price of resources needed to produce the good.
    e. none of the above

13. Five dollars is the equilibrium price for good Z. At a price of $2, there is
    a. a shortage.
    b. surplus.
    c. excess supply.
    d. aggregate demand.

14. If supply rises by a greater amount than demand rises,
    a. equilibrium price rises and equilibrium quantity falls.
    b. equilibrium price falls and equilibrium quantity falls.
    c. equilibrium price rises and equilibrium quantity rises.
    d. equilibrium price falls and equilibrium quantity rises.

15. If supply rises and demand is constant,
    a. equilibrium price rises and equilibrium quantity falls.
    b. equilibrium price falls and equilibrium quantity falls.
    c. equilibrium price rises and equilibrium quantity rises.
    d. equilibrium price falls and equilibrium quantity rises.

True-False
Write a "T" or "F" after each statement.

16. One of the effects of a price ceiling is that quantity supplied is greater than quantity demanded. ____

17. Demand is more important to the determination of market price than supply. ____

18. At the equilibrium price for good X, good X is scarce. ____

19. "Supply" is a specific amount of a good, such as 50 units of good Y. ____

20. There is a tendency for price to rise when the quantity demanded of a good is greater than the quantity supplied. ____

Fill in the Blank
Write the correct word in the blank.

21. As price rises, quantity demanded _____ and quantity supplied _____.

22. A _____ is any arrangement by which people exchange goods and services.

23. If Matt's demand for motorcycles rises as his income falls, then motorcycles are a(n)
    _____ good for Matt.

24. If demand rises more than supply falls, then equilibrium quantity _____.

25. At equilibrium, the quantity demanded of a good _____ the quantity supplied of the
    good.

26. Suppose you live in New York City and are required to rent the furniture in an apartment before you
    can rent the apartment. This is called a _____ - _____ sale.

Chapter 4
Supply and Demand: Applications

What This Chapter Is About
In the last chapter you learned the basic theory of supply and demand. You learned what a demand curve is, what factors will shift it right and left, what a supply curve is, what factors will shift it right and left, and so on. The theory of supply and demand is worth little unless you can apply it. That is what we do in this chapter. We present a series of applications of supply and demand.

Key Concepts in the Chapter
    a.   law of demand
    b.   law of supply
    c.   nonprice rationing device
    d.   minimum wage
    e.   price floor
    f.   price ceiling

- The **law of demand** states that price and quantity demanded are inversely related, *ceteris paribus*.
- The **law of supply** states that price and quantity supplied are directly related, *ceteris paribus*.
- Just as price can serve as a rationing device, so can other things. These other things we call **nonprice rationing devices**. First-come-first-served (FCFS) is a nonprice rationing device.
- The **minimum wage** is the lowest wage a worker can be paid. The minimum wage is an example of a price floor.
- The **price floor** is a government-mandated minimum price below which legal trades cannot be made.
- A **price ceiling** is a government-mandated maximum price above which legal trades cannot be made.

Review Questions

1. The tuition students pay at University X (T_1) is lower than the equilibrium tuition (T_E). If the tuition students pay remains constant, and demand to attend University X rises, what do you predict will happen to the requirements for admission? Explain your answer.

2. How do third-party medical payments end up raising the price of certain medical procedures?

3. How would kidneys (for transplants) be rationed in a free market?

4. Demand for housing rises by the same amount in regions 1 and 2 of the country. However, house prices rise more in region 1 than 2. What could explain this?

5. A university charges a below-equilibrium price for student parking. Might this cause students to be late to class? Explain your answer.

6. There is freeway congestion on Interstate 5 at 8 a.m. on Monday morning. What are three solutions to the problem of freeway congestion at this time?

7. Why might some people argue for a price ceiling or price floor?

8. Will patients pay more for health care if they have the right to sue their provider than if they don't have the right to sue? Explain your answer.

9. In the text it was argued that people pay for good weather. How do they pay for good weather?

10. Why might there be a shortage of some college classes but not others?

Problems

1. Use the law of demand to explain why Yvonne loses her temper with her mother but not with her father.

2. Older people tend to drive more slowly than younger people. For example, a 68-year-old retired person may drive more slowly than a working 32-year-old person. Some people say this is because as people age, their reflexes slow down, their eyesight becomes less clear, and so on. All this may be true. Still, might there be an explanation that has to do with the price of driving? If so, what is this explanation?

3. Suppose the equilibrium tuition at college X is $2,000 a semester, but students only pay $800 a semester. The state taxpayers pay the $1,200 difference. Do you think professors will teach differently knowing their students paid a below-equilibrium tuition instead of the equilibrium tuition? Why or why not?

4. Richard Posner states, "The law of demand doesn't operate just on goods with explicit prices. Unpopular teachers sometimes try to increase enrollment by raising the average grade of the students in their courses, thereby reducing the price of the course to the student." In other words, unpopular teachers give away grades, thus becoming more popular. Do you think the same holds, with necessary changes, for unpopular people? Do unpopular people try to change the price of being around them? Or are they unpopular because the price they charge to be around them is too high?

5. Under what condition will the decriminalization of marijuana lead to an unchanged price for marijuana? (You can assume that decriminalizing marijuana changes both the demand for and supply of marijuana.)

6. Some people argue that an increase in the minimum wage will lead to a large cutback in the number of unskilled workers employed, while others argue that it will lead to only a small cutback in the number of unskilled workers employed. Are the two groups of people arguing over a change in direction or a change in magnitude?

7. "The same number of kidneys will be forthcoming for transplants no matter what the price paid for a kidney." For this statement to be true, what must the supply curve of kidneys look like?

8. Although we did not explicitly cover the next question in the text, try to answer it: Why does a candy bar sell for the same price (or nearly the same price) everywhere in the country, but houses do not?

9. Jones has tried to sell his car for six months. No buyers. Does Jones have a really bad car that no one wants to buy?

10. "Professors in economics, sociology, and biology all lecture, grade papers, meet with students, and so on. It follows, then, that economists and sociologists should be paid the same dollar salary." What does the person who makes this statement forget, overlook, or ignore?

What May Have Been Overlooked?
In each of the statements below, something may have been overlooked or ignored. Identify what may have been overlooked or ignored.

1. The higher the demand for something, the greater the quantity demanded.

2. I think how I behave is independent of the setting that I am in. I act the same way no matter what the setting.

3. If house prices rise by 10 percent in city A, then they will probably rise by the same percentage in city B.

4. The rock band has the best interest of its fans in mind. It knows it can charge $80 a ticket, but it charges only $20 a ticket so that its fans won't have to pay so much.

5. If my university doesn't charge for student parking, then I am definitely better off than I would be if it did charge for student parking.

6. The tuition at Harvard is very high, so Harvard must be charging the equilibrium tuition to students. Still, Harvard uses such things as GPA, SAT and ACT scores for admission purposes. It must be wrong that these nonprice rationing devices (GPA, etc.) are only used by colleges and universities that charge below-equilibrium tuition.

7. If a good doesn't have a money price, it has no price at all.

Multiple Choice
Circle the correct answer.

1. There is no toll charge to drive on freeway A. If there is freeway congestion at 9 a.m., there will be greater freeway congestion at 11 a.m. if
    a. the demand to drive on the freeway is the same at both times.
    b. the demand to drive on the freeway at 11 a.m. is less than the demand to drive on the freeway at 9 a.m.
    c. the demand to drive on the freeway at 9 a.m. is greater than the demand to drive on the freeway at 11 a.m.
    d. fewer people carpool at 11 a.m. than at 9 a.m.
    e. none of the above

2. If goods are not rationed according to price, it follows that
    a.   they won't get rationed at all.
    b.   something will ration the goods.
    c.   first-come-first-served will necessarily be the rationing device.
    d.   there will be surpluses in the market.
    e.   none of the above

3. Market X can be divided into two submarkets, A and B. The supply in each submarket is the same, but
    the demand in A is greater than the demand in B. If submarket B is in equilibrium, it follows that
    a.   A is in equilibrium.
    b.   there is a shortage in A.
    c.   there is a surplus in A.
    d.   there is a shortage in B only if there is a surplus in A.
    e.   none of the above

4. The demand to attend a certain college is represented by a downward-sloping demand curve. The
    supply of spots at the college is represented by a vertical supply curve. At the tuition that students are
    charged, there is a shortage of spots at the college. If the demand to attend the college falls, but the
    tuition stays constant, if follow that the
    a.   GPA required to attend the college will probably rise.
    b.   GPA required to attend the college will probably fall.
    c.   SAT score required to attend the college will probably not change.
    d.   a and c
    e.   There is not enough information to answer the question.

5. Buying is separated from paying by
    a.   a third party
    b.   when demand is higher than supply
    c.   when taxes are applied to the production of a good
    d.   only in the housing market

6. If the minimum wage is the same as the equilibrium wage, then
    a.   there will be a shortage of labor.
    b.   there will be a surplus of labor.
    c.   quantity demanded of labor will equal quantity supplied of labor.
    d.   fewer people will be working than if the minimum wage were lower than the equilibrium wage.
    e.   none of the above

7. If there is a price ceiling in the kidney (available for transplant) market , and the price ceiling is lower
    than the equilibrium price, it follows that
    a.   the supply of kidneys will be vertical.
    b.   the quantity demanded of kidneys will be greater than it would be at equilibrium price.
    c.   the quantity demanded of kidneys will be smaller than it would be at equilibrium price.
    d.   a and b
    e.   a and c

8. The recording industry runs a television ad showing all the people in the industry that are hurt by
    music piracy. This is an attempt to:
    a.   raise the price of music piracy.
    b.   lower the demand for music piracy.
    c.   lower the quantity supplied of songs.
    d.   raise the demand for music piracy.
    e.   none of the above

9. A seller's minimum price for providing a good rises. It follows that
    a.   the supply curve does not change.
    b.   the supply curve shifts upward and to the left.
    c.   the supply curve shifts downward and to the right.
    d.   equilibrium price will end up falling.
    e.   b and d

10. The supply for sociologists and economists is the same, but the demand for sociologists is higher. If
    both sociologists and economists are paid the same salary, it follows that
    a.   there is a shortage of sociologists.
    b.   there is a surplus of economists.
    c.   there is neither a shortage of, nor surplus of, sociologists or economists.
    d.   a and b
    e.   There is not enough information to answer the question.

11. If there is freeway congestion at 8 a.m., we can reduce (or eliminate) the congestion by
    a.   building more freeways.
    b.   raising the price to drive on the freeway at 8 a.m.
    c.   giving people an incentive to carpool.
    d.   a and b
    e.   a, b, and c

12. If parking spots on campus were auctioned to the highest bidder,
    a.   the closest spots to buildings would probably fetch the highest prices.
    b.   the people with the lowest time costs would park the closest to the buildings.
    c.   there would always be shortages.
    d.   a and b
    e.   a, b, and c

13. The university offers "free" seat cushions to any football fan that will arrive at least an hour before the
    game starts. It is correct to say that these cushions are offered at
    a.   zero price.
    b.   zero money price.
    c.   zero nominal price.
    d.   either a or b
    e.   none of the above

14. Aisle seats on commercial airplanes are priced the same as window seats. If the demand for aisle seats
    is greater than the demand for window seats, the supply of each kind of seat is the same, and the
    window-seat market is in equilibrium, it follows that
    a.   the aisle-seat market is in equilibrium, too.
    b.   there is a shortage of aisle seats.
    c.   there is a surplus of aisle seats.
    d.   There is not enough information to answer the question.

15. The price of speeding (on a highway) is equal to the price of a speeding ticket times the probability of
    being caught speeding. If the demand curve for speeding is downward-sloping, it follows that
    a.   a higher probability of getting caught speeding will reduce speeding.
    b.   a higher ticket price will reduce speeding.
    c.   a lower ticket price combined with a higher probability of getting caught speeding will reduce
         speeding.
    d.   a and b
    e.   a, b, and c

True–False
Write a "T" or "F" after each statement.

16. The higher the demand to attend a given college or university, the higher its equilibrium tuition, *ceteris paribus*. ____

17. If there is a price ceiling in the kidney market, and the price ceiling is below the equilibrium price for a kidney, there will be a shortage of kidneys available for transplant. ____

18. If both A and B are bicycles, but A can be resold and B cannot, then the demand for A is likely to be higher than the demand for B, *ceteris paribus*. ____

19. Law 1 gives tenants three months to vacate an apartment, and Law 2 gives tenants six months. Apartment rent is likely to be higher under Law 1. ____

20. The price of pencils is more likely to be the same everywhere than the price of houses. ____

Fill in the Blank
Write the correct word in the blank.

21. At a given price, the greater demand is, the greater _____ _____ is.

22. If there is good weather in City X and bad weather in City Y, and everything is the same about the two cities except the weather, the demand to live in City X will be _____ than the demand to live in City Y.

23. First-come-first-served is a _____ _____ device.

24. NCAA rules often end up raising a colleges _____ _____ signing a college athlete.

25. John earns $100 an hour and Bill earns $20 an hour. If it takes time to make friends, then the _____ price of friendship is higher and, *ceteris paribus*, _____ will make more friends.

Chapter 5
Macroeconomic Measurements, Part I: Prices and Unemployment

What This Chapter Is About
There are many variables that economists measure—the price level, unemployment, gross domestic product (GDP), real gross domestic product (Real GDP), the economic growth rate, and so on. In this chapter we begin to discuss *how* economists measure certain variables. We focus on the price level and unemployment in this chapter; in the next chapter, we focus on GDP and Real GDP.

Key Concepts in the Chapter
a. price level
b. base year
c. nominal income
d. real income
e. inflation
f. unemployment rate
g. frictional unemployment
h. structural unemployment
i. natural unemployment

- The **price level** is the weighted average of the prices of all goods and services. Sometimes it is easier to think of the price level as an average price. For example, suppose the price of good A is $10, the price of good B is $20, and the price of good C is $30. The average price (of these three goods) is $20. In a large economy, there are many goods and services and each sells for a certain price. The average of all the prices of all the goods and services is the price level.
- The **base year** is one year in which all other years are measured up against. It is a benchmark year.
- **Nominal income** is current-dollar income. For example, suppose Suzanne earns an annual income of $60,000. This is her nominal income.
- **Real income** is one's nominal income adjusted for price changes.
- **Inflation** is defined as an increase in the price level. In a later chapter, you will learn about two kinds of inflation—one-shot inflation and continued inflation. In this chapter, we simply define inflation and show how the inflation rate is measured.
- The **unemployment rate** refers to the percentage of the civilian labor force that is unemployed.
- **Frictional unemployment** is a type of unemployment. A person who is frictionally unemployed is an unemployed person who has transferable skills. For example, suppose Joe was just fired from his job as an auto factory worker. If there is another auto factory that is hiring factory workers, then Joe has skills that can be easily transferred to another job.
- **Structural unemployment** is a type of unemployment. A person who is structurally unemployed is an unemployed person who does not have transferable skills. He or she will have to acquire some additional training to get a job. Again, suppose Joe was just fired from his job as an auto factory worker. If the only companies that are hiring currently are computer companies, then Joe may not have the skills necessary to do this kind of work. He is structurally unemployed, and will have to acquire new work skills before he gets a job with a computer company.
- **Natural unemployment** is the sum of frictional unemployment and structural unemployment. The natural unemployment rate is the sum of the frictional and structural unemployment rates. For example, suppose the frictional unemployment rate is 2 percent and the structural unemployment rate is 3 percent. It follows that the natural unemployment rate is 5 percent. When the economy is operating at the natural unemployment rate, full employment is said to exist.

Review Questions

1. What is the relationship between the price level and a price index?

2. Is the consumer price index (CPI) a reflection of the prices of all goods and services produced and purchased in an economy? Explain your answer.

3. If the CPI in a given year is 132, what does this mean?

4. Smith and Jones have the same nominal income, but they live in different countries. Does it follow that they have the same real income? Explain your answer.

5. Steve earned $40,000 income in 1987 and Jeff earned $40,000 in 2003. Was $40,000 in 2003 the same as $40,000 in 1987? Explain your answer.

6. Explain how the CPI is calculated.

7. What is the difference between the civilian noninstitutional population and the civilian labor force?

8. If the unemployment rate is 5 percent, it does not follow that the employment rate is 95 percent. Explain why.

9. What are the four classifications of unemployed persons?

10. What is the difference between a reentrant and a new entrant.

11. Why aren't discouraged workers considered unemployed?

12. Give an example of someone who is structurally unemployed.

Problems

1. In the table (that follows) we have identified current-year prices, base-year prices, and the marketbasket.

Market Basket	Current-year prices (per item)	Base-year prices (per item)
10X	$1.22	$1.10
15Y	$1.66	$1.16
33Z	$3.45	$2.55

What is the CPI for the current year?

2. The CPI was 140.3 in 1992 and 177.1 in 2001. What was the percentage change in prices during the time period 1992-2001?

3. Nominal income is $50,000 and the CPI is 143. What does real income equal?

4. Rebecca's income increased by 20 percent over the last year and prices increased by 2 percent. Did Rebecca's real income rise? Explain your answer.

5. Stacy earned $10,000 in 1967. If the CPI was 33.4 in 1967 and 177.1 in 2001, what was $10,000 equivalent to in 2001?

6. Fill in the numbers missing from the table that follows.

Category	Number of persons
Civilian noninstitutional population	200
Employed	100
Civilian labor force	120
Unemployment rate	
Persons unemployed	
Persons not in the labor force	

7. If the number of persons not in the labor force is 100, persons in the civilian labor force is 200, persons employed is 180, and persons unemployed is 20, then what is the labor force participation rate?

8. How does the labor force participation rate differ from the employment rate?

9. If you know the number of unemployed persons, job losers, and reentrants, is it possible to compute the number of job leavers? Explain your answer.

10. If the natural unemployment rate is 4.5 percent and the structural unemployment rate is 2.1 percent, is it possible to compute the cyclical unemployment rate? Explain your answer.

What Is the Question?
Identify the question for each of the answers that follow.

1. The consumer price index.

2. Take the nominal income and divide it by the CPI. Then take the quotient and multiply it by 100.

3. The number of persons employed plus the number of persons unemployed.

4. The natural unemployment rate minus the frictional unemployment rate.

5. This person is not considered unemployed (by the government), even though many people think this person should be considered unemployed.

6. The cyclical unemployment rate.

7. The first step is to subtract the CPI in the earlier year from the CPI in the later year. The second step is to divide by the CPI in the earlier year. The third step is to multiply by 100.

8. This happens if the CPI rises by more than your nominal income.

9. This person did at least one hour of work as a paid employee during the survey week.

10. This person quit his job.

11. This person got fired but doesn't (currently) have transferable skills.

Multiple Choice
Circle the correct answer.

1. If the CPI was 72.6 in 1979 and 144.5 in 1993, by what percentage did prices rise during the period 1979-1999?
    a. 100.3 percent
    b. 160.7 percent
    c. 99.0 percent
    d. 15.09 percent
    e. none of the above

2. Good X sold for $40 in 1945. The CPI in 1945 was 18.0 and the CPI in 1999 was 166.6. What was the price of good X in 1999 dollars?
    a. $233.88
    b. $243.76
    c. $370.22
    d. $211.89
    e. none of the above

3. A _____ is a person who was employed in the civilian labor force and quit his or her job.
    a. new entrant
    b. reentrant
    c. job leaver
    d. job fixer
    e. none of the above

4. The answer is: "a person employed in the civilian labor force who quits his or her job." The question is:
    a. Who is a job loser?
    b. Who is an entrant?
    c. Who is a reentrant?
    d. Who is a job leaver?
    e. Who is a discouraged worker?

5. A _____ is a person who has never held a full-time job for two weeks or longer and is now in the civilian labor force looking for a job.
   a. new entrant
   b. reentrant
   c. job fixer
   d. job leaver
   e. job loser

6. Which of the following statements is false?
   a. A discouraged worker is not counted as an unemployed worker.
   b. The frictional unemployment rate is less than the natural unemployment rate.
   c. The natural unemployment rate is greater than the structural unemployment rate.
   d. a and b
   e. none of the above

7. Of all the categories of unemployment, most unemployed persons fall into the category of being a
   a. reentrant
   b. new entrant
   c. job leaver
   d. job loser
   e. none of the above

8. If there are 35 job losers, 13 job leavers, 14 reentrants, and 10 new entrants, then there are _____ frictionally unemployed persons.
   a. 72
   b. 35
   c. 48
   d. 62
   e. There is not enough information to answer the question.

9. The number of employed persons plus the number of unemployed persons equals the number of persons
   a. in the total population.
   b. in the civilian noninstitutional population.
   c. in the civilian labor force.
   d. not in the labor force.
   e. none of the above

10. If we subtract the number of people not in the labor force from the civilian noninstitutional population, we get the number of people in the
    a. ranks of the unemployed.
    b. civilian labor force.
    c. ranks of the employed.
    d. ranks of discouraged workers.
    e. none of the above

11. _____ is an increase in the price level and is usually measured on an annual basis.
    a. Deflation
    b. Inflation
    c. Stagflation
    d. Economic growth
    e. none of the above

12. If your nominal income rises faster than prices, it follows that
    a. there is no inflation.
    b. there is deflation.
    c. your real income falls.
    d. your real income rises.
    e. b and c

13. The CPI contains _____ goods and services than the GDP implicit price deflator.
    a. more
    b. fewer
    c. the same number of
    d. higher-quality
    e. lower-quality

14. The civilian noninstitutional population is equal to _____ plus _____.
    a. persons not in the labor force; employed persons
    b. employed persons; unemployed persons
    c. reentrants; entrants
    d. persons not in the labor force; persons in the civilian labor force
    e. the total population; reentrants

15. The labor force participation rate is equal to the
    a. civilian labor force divided by the civilian noninstitutional population.
    b. number of employed persons divided by the civilian labor force.
    c. unemployment rate minus the employment rate.
    d. number of entrants plus number of reentrants.
    e. none of the above

True-False
Write a "T" or "F" after each statement.

16. The frictional unemployment rate minus the cyclical unemployment rate equals the natural unemployment rate. _____

17. If the economy is operating at the natural unemployment rate, there is full employment. _____

18. The price level is the weighted average of the prices of goods and services in the economy. _____

19. If the unemployment rate is 8 percent and the natural unemployment rate is 5 percent, then the cyclical unemployment rate is 3 percent. _____

20. The CPI is calculated by the Bureau of Labor Statistics. _____

Fill in the Blank
Write the correct word in the blank.

21. The _____ _____ is equal to the cyclical unemployment rate plus the natural unemployment rate.

22. The CPI is a _____ _____.

23. Nominal income adjusted for price changes is _____ _____.

24. As the optimal search time rises, the unemployment rate _____.

25. The _____ _____ is a benchmark year.

Chapter 6
Macroeconomic Measurements, Part II: GDP and Real GDP

What This Chapter Is About
In the last chapter we discussed a few macroeconomic measurements, such as the price level and unemployment. In this chapter we continue with the discussion of macroeconomic measurements. Here we discuss gross domestic product (GDP) and real gross domestic product (Real GDP).

Key Concepts in the Chapter
- a.   GDP
- b.   Real GDP
- c.   business cycle

- **GDP (gross domestic product)** is the total market value of all final goods and services produced annually within a country's borders.
- **Real GDP** is GDP adjusted for price changes.
- A **business cycle** refers to the recurrent swings in Real GDP.

Review Questions

1.   GDP is defined as the total market value of all final goods and services produced annually within a country's borders. Give an example to illustrate what "total market value" means.

2.   Give an example of a final good and of an intermediate good.

3.   Sales of used goods are not considered when computing GDP. Explain why.

4.   Why aren't financial transactions counted in GDP?

5.   What are the three components of consumption?

6.   What is fixed investment? How does it differ from inventory investment?

7.   Why aren't government transfer payments counted in GDP?

8.   What does national income equal?

9.   What is net domestic product?

10. How does personal income differ from national income?

11. How does disposable income differ from personal income?

12. If GDP rises, does it follow that Real GDP rises, too? Explain your answer.

13. How is economic growth measured?

Problems

1. Good X is made with intermediate goods A and B. The market value of A is $10, the market value of B is $13, and the market value of X is $23. Which of the three dollar amounts goes into the computation of GDP? Explain your answer.

2. The following activities (shown in the table) take place in a tiny economy.

Item	Market value of item
Nancy cleans her house.	$40.00
Bob buys illegal drugs at the corner of 5th St.	$400.00
Smithies receives a social security check written out for $654.32.	$654.32
Karen buys 100 shares of stock Z.	$1,255.00
Mario buys a used car from Nanette.	$4,099.00
Bob mows his lawn.	$50.00
Carl produces and sells shoes.	$100.00

What does GDP equal?

3. Is it possible to compute GDP using the expenditure approach if you do not know the value of the purchases of new residential housing but do know the value of fixed investment? Explain your answer.

4. Using the expenditure approach to measuring GDP, what does GDP equal?

5. What will cause GDP to fall?

6. Using the table that follows, compute GDP.

Item	$ Value (in millions)
Durable goods	$400
Inventory investment	30
Purchases of new residential housing	100
Nondurable goods	300
Services	100
Purchases of new capital goods	50
Fixed investment	150
Inventory investment	25
Federal government purchases	80
Government transfer payments	20
Net interest on the public debt	30
State government purchases	90
Local government purchases	70
Exports	100
Imports	190
Income taxes	80
Consumption	800
Net exports	-90
Investment	175

What does GDP equal?

7. Using the table below, compute national income.

Item	$ Value (in millions)
Income taxes	$30
Net interest	20
Corporate profits	40
Consumption	300
Rental income	100
Proprietors' income	200
Compensation of employees	700
Investment	200
Excise taxes	10

What does national income equal?

8. Using the table that follows, compute personal income.

Item	$ Value (in millions)
National income	$1,200
Undistributed corporate profits	300
Social insurance taxes	160
Corporate profits taxes	40
Inventory investment	90
Government purchases	240
Transfer payments	200

What does personal income equal?

9. Using the table that follows, compute both GDP and Real GDP.

Quantities of various goods produced	Price of good in the current year	Price of good in the base year
100 X	$1	$1
200 Y	$2	$1
300 Z	$7	$3

What does GDP equal?

What does Real GDP equal?

10. Fill in the last column in the table that follows.

GDP	Population	Per capita GDP
$1,200 billion	100 million	
$500 billion	67 million	
$3,000 billion	50 million	

11. Use the terms (a) GDP, (b) income earned from the rest of the world, and (c) income earned by the rest of the world to define GNP.

12. Use the terms (a) GNP, (b) income earned from the rest of the world, and (c) income earned by the rest of the world to define GDP.

13. If you know the dollar amount of the capital consumption allowance and net domestic product, is it possible to compute GDP? Explain your answer.

14. If the first peak of a business cycle is in March, and the second peak of the business cycle is in July, is it possible to identify (in months) the length of the recovery? Explain your answer.

15. If the contraction of a business cycle is 12 months, the recovery is 13 months, and the expansion is 12 months, then how long after the first peak of business cycle does the second peak come?

What Is Wrong?
In each of the statements below, something is wrong. Identify what is wrong in the space provided.

1. The expansion phase of a business cycle is generally longer than the recovery stage.

2. A stock variable makes little sense without some time period specified.

3. Fixed investment includes business purchases of new capital goods, inventory investment, and purchases of new residential housing.

4. GDP = C + I + G + EX + IM

5. Net domestic product is equal to GDP minus capital consumption allowance. Another name for capital consumption allowance is capital good.

6. A business cycle is measured from trough to peak.

7. The largest expenditure component of GDP is government purchases.

What is the Question?
Identify the question for each of the answers that follow.

1. GDP divided by population.

2. Five phases: peak, contraction, trough, recovery, and expansion.

3. First, subtract Real GDP in the earlier year from Real GDP in the current year. Second, divide by Real GDP. Third, multiply by 100.

4. National income minus undistributed corporate profits minus social insurance taxes minus corporate profits taxes plus transfer payments.

5. Personal income minus personal taxes.

Multiple Choice
Circle the correct answer.

1. Gross Domestic Product (GDP) is
    a. the total market value of all final goods and services produced annually within a country's borders.
    b. the total market value of all final and intermediate goods and services produced annually within a country's borders.
    c. NDP minus capital consumption allowance.
    d. personal income plus taxes plus disposable income.
    e. none of the above

2. Which of the following illustrates double counting?
    a. counting the value of intermediate goods only
    b. counting the value of intermediate goods and final goods
    c. counting the value of final goods only
    d. counting the value of used car sales when measuring GDP
    e. c and d

3. Which of the following is an intermediate good?
    a. mustard on a ham sandwich sold at a restaurant
    b. tires on a new car
    c. a computer sold online
    d. a book sold at a bookstore
    e. a and b

4. The income approach to measuring GDP takes the sums of
    a. consumption, net exports, and government purchases.
    b. personal income, proprietors' income, investment, and net exports.
    c. consumption, government purchases, investment, and net exports.
    d. national income, exports, and imports.
    e. none of the above

5. Government purchases consist of the total dollar amount(s) spent by the
    a. federal government only.
    b. state government only.
    c. federal and state governments.
    d. local government only.
    e. federal, state, and local governments.

6. Leisure is
    a. a good that is counted in GDP.
    b. a bad that is counted in GDP.
    c. a good that is not counted in GDP.
    d. equal to personal income minus taxes minus savings.
    e. c and d

7. Which of the following is often the smallest figure?
    a. GDP
    b. government purchases
    c. net exports
    d. investment
    e. consumption

8. Which of the following statements is true?
   a. Real GDP is equal to GDP multiplied by the price level.
   b. Disposable income is equal to personal income minus consumption.
   c. Net exports is equal to exports plus imports.
   d. A social security check is an example of a government transfer payment.
   e. a and d

9. If there is a decrease in inventories, it follows that
   a. fixed investment falls.
   b. new residential housing purchases fall.
   c. capital investment falls.
   d. inventory investment rises.
   e. none of the above

10. Which of the following statements is true?
    a. Net exports (for the U.S.) is always positive.
    b. GDP = C + I + G + EX
    c. A business cycle cannot be longer than 18 months.
    d. Exports plus imports is net exports.
    e. none of the above

11. Which of the following is not counted in GDP?
    a. an illegal drug transaction
    b. the production of telephones
    c. the production of shoes
    d. own-home housework
    e. a and d

12. An example of a government transfer payment is
    a. a social security check.
    b. taxes paid on income earned.
    c. excise taxes.
    d. personal income.
    e. none of the above

13. Consumption includes
    a. durable goods and services.
    b. nondurable goods.
    c. inventory investment minus government purchases.
    d. net exports minus government purchases.
    e. a and b

14. Real GDP is equal to
    a. GDP minus NDP.
    b. the sum of current-year quantities multiplied by base-year prices.
    c. the sum of current-year quantities multiplied by current-year prices.
    d. (base-year prices multiplied by current-year prices) minus current-year quantities.
    e. none of the above

15. National income equals
    a. the sum of resource or factor payments.
    b. compensation of employees plus proprietors' income plus rental income plus net interest.
    c. personal income plus personal taxes.
    d. disposable income at current-year prices.
    e. a and b

True False
Write a "T" or "F" after each statement.

16. In year 1, the price index was 127 and GDP was $7,000 billion. It follows that Real GDP in year 1 was approximately $6,281 billion. _____

17. Real GDP is never measured in base-year prices. _____

18. The base year is the year in which prices are the lowest. _____

19. Economic growth has occurred when Real GDP has risen over the year. _____

20. The typical business cycle is measured from expansion to trough. _____

Fill in the Blank
Write the correct word in the blank.

21. A recession is sometimes defined as _____ or more consecutive quarters of falling Real GDP.

22. A business cycle has _____ phases.

23. The bottom of the contraction is called a _____.

24. GDP is a _____ variable.

25. _____ is the sum of fixed investment and inventory investment.

Chapter 7
Aggregate Demand and Aggregate Supply

What This Chapter Is About
This is one of the most important chapters in the text. It introduces the AD-AS model, or framework, which we will use for the duration of our study of macroeconomics. Just as economists say there are two sides to a market (a demand side and a supply side), so are there two sides to an economy. We discuss each side in this chapter, then put the two sides together to discuss the economy. Our time-period for studying the economy in this chapter is the short run.

Key Concepts in the Chapter
a. aggregate demand
b. real wage
c. short-run aggregate supply
d. short-run equilibrium
e. natural real GDP
f. long-run aggregate supply curve

- **Aggregate demand** is the quantity demanded of all goods and services at different price levels. Don't think of aggregate demand as a particular dollar amount. It is a series of quantities demanded (of Real GDP) at various price levels.
- **Real wage** is the nominal wage (or money wage) adjusted for price changes. In this chapter the real wage is equal to the nominal wage divided by the price level.
- **Short-run aggregate supply** is the quantity supplied of all goods and services at different price levels. Don't think of short-run aggregate supply as a particular dollar amount of goods and services. It is a series of quantities supplied (of Real GDP) at various price levels.
- **Short-run equilibrium** is the condition that exists in the economy when the quantity demanded of Real GDP equals the (short-run) quantity supplied of Real GDP. This condition is met where the aggregate demand curve intersects the short-run aggregate supply curve.
- **Natural Real GDP** is the Real GDP that is produced at the level of natural unemployment rate. It is the Real GDP that is produced when the economy is in long-run equilibrium.
- The **long-run aggregate supply (LRAS) curve** is a vertical line at the level of Natural Real GDP. It represents the output the economy produces when wages and prices have adjusted to their (final) equilibrium levels and neither producers nor workers have any relevant misperceptions.

Review Questions

1. Why do aggregate demand curves slope downward?

2. What is the difference between a change in the quantity demanded of Real GDP and a change in aggregate demand?

3. What are the components of total expenditures (or total spending)?

4. Will a lower price level change aggregate demand? Explain your answer.

5. Consumption will change if certain factors change. What are the factors that can change consumption?

6. What are the factors that can change investment?

7. What are the factors that can change net exports?

8. Outline the details of the sticky-wages explanation for the upward-sloping SRAS curve.

9. Outline the details of the worker-misperceptions explanation for the upward-sloping SRAS curve.

10. What factors can change SRAS?

Problems

1. Fill in the blank spaces in the table.

If...	AD curve shifts to the (right or left?)
consumption rises	
investment rises	
exports rise	
imports rise	
government purchases rise	
consumption falls	
net exports rise	

2. Fill in the blank spaces in the table.

If...	SRAS curve shifts to the (right or left?)
wage rates rise	
prices of nonlabor inputs fall	
productivity increases	
adverse supply shock	
beneficial supply shock	
wage rates fall	

3. Fill in the blank spaces in the table.

Factor	How does the factor change affect C, I, G, EX, and/or IM?
wealth rises	
individuals expect higher (future) prices	
individuals expect higher (future) income	
interest rate rises	
income taxes fall	
businesses expect higher (future) sales	
business taxes rise	
foreign real national income falls	
dollar appreciates	
dollar depreciates	

4. Fill in the blank spaces in the table.

Factor	Does the AD curve shift? (right, left, no change)	Does the SRAS curve shift? (right, left, no change)	Is there a change in the price level? (up, down, no change)	Is there a change in Real GDP? (up, down, no change)	Is there a change in the unemployment rate? (up, down, no change)
interest rate falls					
wage rates rise					
productivity rises					
adverse supply shock					
wealth falls					
businesses expect lower (future) sales					
dollar appreciates					
prices of nonlabor inputs rise					
beneficial supply shock					
wealth rises					
dollar depreciates					
wage rates fall					

5. Diagrammatically represent short-run equilibrium.

Price Level

Real GDP

6. Diagrammatically represent long-run equilibrium.

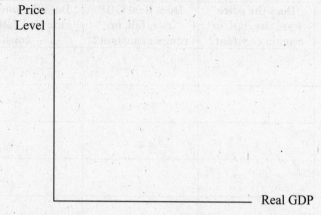

7. Diagrammatically represent an increase in aggregate demand that is greater than an increase in short-run aggregate supply.

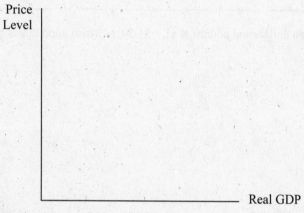

8. Diagrammatically represent a decrease in aggregate demand that is greater than a decrease in short-run aggregate supply.

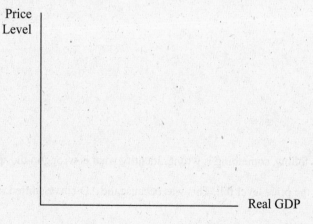

9. Fill in the blank spaces in the table.

Suppose...	Does the price level rise, fall, or remain constant?	Does Real GDP rise, fall, or remain constant?	Does the unemployment rate rise, fall, or remain constant?
AD rises			
AD rises by more than SRAS falls			
SRAS falls			
SRAS rises by the same amount as AD rises			
SRAS rises			
AD falls			

10. If the exchange rate between dollars and pounds is £1 = $1.50, a British good that is priced at £150 costs how many dollars?

11. If the exchange rate between dollars and pounds is £1 = $1.50, a U.S. good that is priced at $300 costs how many pounds?

What Is Wrong?
In each of the statements that follow, something is wrong. Identify what is wrong in the space provided.

1. Real GDP increased and the price level fell. This was because the AD curve shifted to the right.

2.   Real GDP and the price level increased. This was because the SRAS curve shifted to the right.

3.   If SRAS increases, the SRAS curve shifts upward and to the left.

4.   The price level increased and Real GDP decreased. This is because the AD curve shifted to the left.

5.   A change in interest rates will affect both consumption and government purchases.

6.   If the dollar appreciates, this means it takes more dollars to buy a unit of foreign currency.

7.   An increase in wealth will raise consumption, aggregate demand, and the price level. It will lower Real GDP.

8.   A decline in interest rates will raise consumption and investment, lower aggregate demand, shift the AD curve left, and raise the price level.

9.   The LRAS curve is vertical at the current level of Real GDP.

10. Long-run equilibrium is at the intersection of the AD curve and the upward-sloping LRAS curve, while short-run equilibrium is at the intersection of the AD curve and the vertical SRAS curve.

11. An increase in the interest rate will lower the demand for loanable funds.

Multiple Choice
Circle the correct answer.

1. If the nominal wage is $100 and the price level (as measured by a price index) is 5.0, it follows that the real wage is
   a. $100.
   b. $20.
   c. $2.50.
   d. $10.
   e. none of the above

2. If wages are sticky, a decline in the price level will
   a. raise the real wage and lower the quantity demanded of labor.
   b. lower the real wage and lower the quantity supplied of labor.
   c. raise the real wage and lower the quantity supplied of labor.
   d. a and b
   e. none of the above

3. Which of the following is consistent with the sticky-wage explanation of the upward-sloping SRAS curve?
   a. The price level rises, the real wage falls, and the quantity demanded of labor declines.
   b. The price level rises, the real wage rises, and the quantity demanded of labor rises.
   c. The price level falls, the real wage rises, and the quantity demanded of labor falls.
   d. The nominal wage rises, the real wage rises, and the quantity demanded and supplied of labor rise.
   e. a and b

4. Aggregate demand increases and short-run aggregate supply decreases by more (than aggregate demand increases). As a result,
   a. the price level rises and Real GDP rises.
   b. the price level falls and Real GDP falls.
   c. the price level rises and Real GDP falls.
   d. the price level falls and Real GDP rises.
   e. none of the above

5. Which of the following is consistent with the worker misperceptions explanation of the upward-sloping SRAS curve?
    a. Workers always overestimate their real wages.
    b. Producers misperceive relative price changes.
    c. Workers initially underestimate changes in their real wages.
    d. Workers correctly perceive real wage changes in the short run but not in the long run.
    e. none of the above

6. Which of the following statements is false?
    a. If exchange rate is $1 = 10 Mexican pesos on Monday and $1 = 8 Mexican pesos on Wednesday, then the dollar has appreciated between Monday and Wednesday.
    b. Real wages are nominal wages divided by the price level.
    c. If the real wage rises, the quantity demanded of labor falls.
    d. A decrease in productivity will shift the SRAS curve to the right.
    e. b and d

7. The economy suffers an adverse supply shock. As a result, in the short run Real GDP will _____ and the price level will _____.
    a. rise; rise
    b. fall; fall
    c. fall; remain constant
    d. fall; rise
    e. rise; fall

8. There is a fall in productivity in the economy. As a result, in the short run Real GDP _____ and the price level _____.
    a. rises; falls
    b. falls; rises
    c. falls; falls
    d. rises; rises
    e. remains constant; remains constant

9. Here is some information: (1) the wage rises, (2) the interest rate rises, (3) any change in AD is greater than any change in SRAS. Based on this information, in the short run Real GDP will _____ and the price level will _____.
    a. rise; rise
    b. fall; rise
    c. fall; fall
    d. rise; fall
    e. remain constant; rise

10. _____ identifies the level of Real GDP the economy produces when wages and prices have adjusted to their (final) equilibrium levels and there are no misperceptions on the part of either producers or workers.
    a. Short-run equilibrium
    b. Disequilibrium
    c. Long-run equilibrium
    d. Equilibrium
    e. none of the above

11. Real GDP rises and the price level falls. This can be brought about by
    a. an increase in AD.
    b. a decrease in AD.
    c. an increase in SRAS.
    d. a decrease in SRAS.
    e. none of the above

12. Real GDP falls and the price level rises. This can be brought about by
    a.   an increase in AD.
    b.   a decrease in AD.
    c.   an increase in SRAS.
    d.   a decrease in SRAS.
    e.   none of the above

13. Real GDP and the price level fall. This can be brought about by
    a.   an increase in AD.
    b.   a decrease in AD.
    c.   'an increase in SRAS.
    d.   a decrease in SRAS.
    e.   none of the above

14. Real GDP and the price level rise. This can be brought about by
    a.   an increase in AD.
    b.   a decrease in AD.
    c.   an increase in SRAS.
    d.   a decrease in SRAS.
    e.   none of the above

15. The components of total expenditures include
    a.   consumption, investment, and government purchases.
    b.   exports and imports.
    c.   national income, personal income, and income taxes.
    d.   wealth, interest rate, and wage rates.
    e.   a and b

True-False
Write a "T" or "F" after each statement.

16. The real-balance effect deals with the change in the purchasing power of dollar-denominated assets that results from a change in the price level. _____

17. An increase in interest rates will raise investment. _____

18. If the dollar depreciates, net exports will rise. _____

19. If the dollar appreciates, exports will fall. _____

20. A rise in wage rates will shift the SRAS curve to the right. _____

Fill in the Blank
Write the correct word in the blank.

21. If the price level rises, the real wage _____.

22. If the nominal wage rises, and the price level is constant, the real wage _____.

23. _____ describes the output produced per unit of input employed over some period of time.

24. If wealth rises, consumption rises, and the _____ curve shifts to the right.

25. As the prices of nonlabor inputs fall, the SRAS curves shifts to the _____.

Chapter 8
The Self-Regulating Economy

What This Chapter Is About

Economists don't all agree as to how the economy works. In this chapter, we present the view of some economists as to how the economy works. For some economists, the economy is self-regulating. This means if the economy is in either a recessionary gap, or in an inflationary gap, it can "heal" itself and move into long-run equilibrium and produce Natural Real GDP.

Key Concepts in the Chapter
a. Say's law
b. recessionary gap
c. inflationary gap
d. wage and price flexibility

- **Say's law** holds that supply creates its own demand. Production creates demand sufficient to purchase all goods and services produced.
- A **recessionary gap** exists in the economy if the economy is producing a Real GDP level that is less than the Natural Real GDP level. Alternatively, a recessionary gap exists if the unemployment rate in the economy is greater than the natural unemployment rate. For example, if the unemployment rate in the economy is 5 percent, and the natural unemployment rate is 4 percent, then the economy is in a recessionary gap.
- An **inflationary gap** exists in the economy if the economy is producing a Real GDP level that is greater than the Natural Real GDP level. Alternatively, an inflationary gap exists if the unemployment rate in the economy is less than the natural unemployment rate. For example, if the unemployment rate in the economy is 3 percent, and the natural unemployment rate is 4 percent, then the economy is in an inflationary gap.
- **Wage and price flexibility** refers to wages and prices adjusting to shortages and surpluses in markets. For example, if there is wage flexibility in the labor market, then if there is a surplus in the labor market, the wage rate will fall; if there is a shortage in the labor market, the wage rate will rise. If wages were inflexible, then it might be the case that a surplus exists in the labor market, but the wage rate does not fall. In this case, the wage rate is inflexible in the downward direction.

Review Questions

1. In a money economy, a person may earn $1,000 a month, but spend only $900 of it on goods and services. In other words, $100 is saved each month. Does Say's law still hold, according to a classical economist? Explain your answer.

2. In the classical view of the credit market, the amount of investment increases as a result of saving increasing. Explain how an increase in saving can lead to more investment.

3. What is the classical position on wages and prices? Are there economists today who take the classical position on wages and prices?

4. What does it mean to say "the economy is self-regulating"?

5. What condition defines a recessionary gap?

6. What condition defines an inflationary gap?

7. If the economy is in a recessionary gap, is the unemployment rate (that exists in the economy) greater than or less than the natural unemployment rate?

8. If the economy is in an inflationary gap, is the unemployment rate (that exists in the economy) greater than or less than the natural unemployment rate?

9. If the economy is in a recessionary gap, is the labor market in shortage, surplus, or equilibrium?

10. If the economy is in an inflationary gap, is the labor market in shortage, surplus, or equilibrium?

11. Explain the process by which a self-regulating economy removes itself from a recessionary gap.

12. Explain the process by which a self-regulating economy removes itself from an inflationary gap.

Problems

1. Fill in the blank spaces in the table.

State of the economy	The labor market is in (shortage, surplus, equilibrium)	The wage rate will (rise, fall, remain unchanged)	The SRAS curve will shift (right, left)
Recessionary gap			
Inflationary gap			
Long-run equilibrium			

2. If the price level is rising, which is more likely: (a) the economy is removing itself from a recessionary gap, or (b) the economy is removing itself from an inflationary gap? Explain your answer.

3. If Real GDP is falling, which is more likely: (a) the economy is removing itself from a recessionary gap, or (b) the economy is removing itself from an inflationary gap? Explain your answer.

4. If Real GDP is rising, which is more likely: a) the economy is removing itself from a recessionary gap, or (b) the economy is removing itself from an inflationary gap? Explain your answer.

5. If the price level is falling, which is more likely: a) the economy is removing itself from a recessionary gap, or (b) the economy is removing itself from an inflationary gap? Explain your answer.

6. Suppose the economy is in long-run equilibrium in Year 1. Then aggregate demand rises. In Year 2 the economy is in long-run equilibrium again. If the economy is self-regulating, is the price level in Year 2 higher than, lower than, or equal to the price level in Year 1? Explain your answer.

7. Suppose the economy is in long-run equilibrium in Year 1. Then aggregate demand falls. In Year 2 the economy is in long-run equilibrium again. If the economy is self-regulating, is the price level in Year 2 higher than, lower than, or equal to the price level in Year 1? Explain your answer.

8. Suppose the economy is in long-run equilibrium in Year 1. Then short-run aggregate supply falls. In Year 2 the economy is in long-run equilibrium again. If the economy is self-regulating, is the price level in Year 2 higher than, lower than, or equal to the price level in Year 1? Explain your answer.

What Is the Question?
Identify the question for each of the answers that follows.

1. These economists believe that Say's law holds in a money economy.

2. (Current) Real GDP is less than Natural Real GDP.

3. The economy is operating at Natural Real GDP.

4. (Current) Real GDP is greater than Natural Real GDP.

5. The economy is operating beyond its institutional production possibilities frontier (PPF).

6. The economy is operating below its institutional production possibilities frontier (PPF).

7. In the long run, the price level is higher, but Real GDP is unchanged.

8. In the long run, the price level is lower, but Real GDP is unchanged.

What Is Wrong?

In each of the statements that follow, something is wrong. Identify what is wrong in the space provided.

1. The economy is initially in long-run equilibrium. Then, aggregate demand rises. In the short run, the price level and Real GDP rise. If the economy is not self regulating, in the long run the price level has risen and Real GDP has been unchanged (from its initial long-run position).

2. The economy is initially in long-run equilibrium. Then, short-run aggregate supply falls. In the short run, the price level and Real GDP rise. If the economy is self regulating, in the long run the price level has fallen back to its original level and Real GDP has been unchanged (from its initial long-run position).

3. The economy is in a recessionary gap if it is operating at the natural unemployment rate.

4. The economy is in an inflationary gap if the unemployment rate is greater than the natural unemployment rate.

5. The diagram (that follows) shows an economy in a recessionary gap.

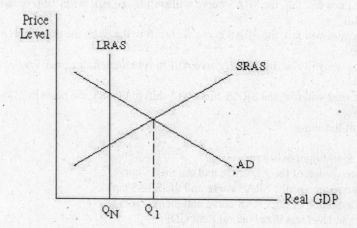

6. If wage rates fall, the SRAS curve shifts to the left.

Multiple Choice
Circle the correct answer.

1. An economy is producing its Natural Real GDP when the rate of unemployment is the
    a. cyclical unemployment rate.
    b. structural unemployment rate.
    c. natural unemployment rate.
    d. frictional unemployment rate.
    e. equal to the natural unemployment rate minus the cyclical unemployment rate.

2. If the SRAS curve intersects the AD curve to the right of Natural Real GDP, the economy is in
    a. a recessionary gap.
    b. an inflationary gap.
    c. a cyclical inflationary gap.
    d. a recession.
    e. an economic expansion.

3. Smith believes the economy is self regulating. Which of the following describes what he believes will happen if the economy is in a recessionary gap?
    a. Wage rates will fall, the SRAS curve will shift to the left, the price level will rise, and Real GDP will fall.
    b. Wage rates will fall, the SRAS curve will shift to the right, the price level will fall, and Real GDP will rise.
    c. Wage rates will rise, the SRAS curve will shift to the left, the price level will rise, and Real GDP will fall.
    d. Wage rates will rise, the SRAS curve will shift to the left, the price level will fall, and Real GDP will rise.
    e. none of the above

4. Jones believes the economy is self regulating. Which of the following describes what she believes will happen if the economy is in an inflationary gap?
    a. Wage rates will fall, the SRAS curve will shift to the left, the price level will rise, and Real GDP will fall.
    b. Wage rates will fall, the SRAS curve will shift to the right, the price level will fall, and Real GDP will rise.
    c. Wage rates will rise, the SRAS curve will shift to the left, the price level will rise, and Real GDP will fall.
    d. Wage rates will rise, the SRAS curve will shift to the left, the price level will fall, and Real GDP will rise.
    e. none of the above

5. Long-run equilibrium exists at
    a. the intersection of the AD curve and the SRAS curve.
    b. the intersection of the SRAS curve and the SRAS curve.
    c. the intersection of the LRAS curve and the AD curve.
    d. an output level less than Natural Real GDP.
    e. c and d

6. According to a Say's law, in a money economy a reduction in consumption spending causes a _____ shift of the saving curve and therefore a _____ in the interest rate.
    a. leftward; rise
    b. leftward; fall
    c. rightward; rise
    d. rightward; fall

7. According to Say's law, there can be
    a. neither a general overproduction nor a general underproduction of goods.
    b. a general overproduction, but not a general underproduction, of goods.
    c. a general underproduction, but not a general overproduction, of goods.
    d. both a general overproduction and a general underproduction of goods.

8. The classical economists argued that
    a. supply today creates supply tomorrow.
    b. wages are inflexible.
    c. interest rates are inflexible.
    d. saving is always greater than investment.
    e. wages and prices are flexible.

9. According to classical economists,
   a. total expenditures rise if consumption falls.
   b. total expenditures fall if consumption rises.
   c. Say's law holds in both a barter economy and in a money economy.
   d. total expenditures remain constant if consumption falls.
   e. c and d

10. The economy is in long-run equilibrium. Then, aggregate demand rises. In the short run,
    a. the price level is higher and Real GDP is lower.
    b. the price level is lower and Real GDP is higher.
    c. both the price level and Real GDP are lower.
    d. both the price level and Real GDP are higher.
    e. There is not enough information to answer the question.

True-False
Write a "T" or "F" after each statement.

11. According to classical economists, Say's law holds in a barter economy but not in a money economy. ____

12. When the economy is in a recessionary gap, there is a shortage in the labor market. ____

13. When the economy is in long-run equilibrium, the unemployment rate is equal to the natural unemployment rate and the Real GDP level is the Natural Real GDP. ____

14. According to classical economists, saving equals investment because the interest rate is rigid. ____

15. A self-regulating economy is one that can remove itself from both inflationary and recessionary gaps. ____

Fill in the Blank
Write the correct word in the blank.

16. If the economy is operating below its institutional PPF, it is in a(an) _____ gap.

17. If the economy is self regulating and in an inflationary gap, wage rates will _____ and the SRAS curve will shift _____.

18. If the economy is self regulating and in a recessionary gap, wage rates will _____ and the SRAS curve will shift _____.

19. The _____ production possibilities frontier lies further to the right than the _____ production possibilities frontier.

20. _____ - _____ is the public policy of not interfering with market activities in the economy.

Chapter 9
Economic Instability: A Critique of the Self-Regulating Economy

What This Chapter Is About
In the last chapter we discussed the self-regulating economy. Not all economists believe the economy is self regulating. Some economists believe that the economy can sometimes be given to instability. In other words, the economy may not remove itself from, say, a recessionary gap. We discuss this position in this chapter.

Key Concepts in the Chapter
    a.   efficiency wages
    b.   consumption function
    c.   autonomous spending
    d.   multiplier
    e.   Keynesian aggregate supply curve

- **Efficiency wages** refer to wage rates above equilibrium levels. For example, if the equilibrium wage rate is $30 an hour, an efficiency wage rate might be $35 an hour. Some economists believe there are solid microeconomic reasons for efficiency wages.
- The **consumption function** (in this chapter) relates consumption spending to disposable income.
- **Autonomous spending** is spending independent of income. For example, if investment spending rises from $40 million to $50 million even if income (in the economy) is constant, this $10 million change in investment spending is referred to as change in autonomous investment spending.
- The **multiplier** is the number that is multiplied by the change in autonomous spending to obtain the change in Real GDP.

Review Questions

1.   Does Keynes believe in Say's law in a money economy? Explain your answer.

2.   According to Keynesians, the economy can get stuck in a recessionary gap. According to them, why might the economy get stuck in a recessionary gap?

3.   What is the Keynesian position on wages and prices?

4.   What are the three simplifying assumptions in the simple Keynesian model?

5.   Write the Keynesian consumption function.

6.   Using the Keynesian consumption function, what will lead to a rise in consumption?

7.   How is the marginal propensity to consume computed?

8.   How is the marginal propensity to save computed?

9.   Explain how the total expenditures (TE) curve is derived.

10. What role does *optimum inventory* play in the Keynesian analysis of the economy?

11. What happens in the economy if TE > TP (TE = total expenditures; TP = total production)?

12. According to Keynesians, can the economy be in equilibrium and in a recessionary gap, too? Explain your answer.

13. What does the multiplier equal?

14. What is the Keynesian position on the ability of the private sector to remove the economy from a recessionary gap?

Problems

1. Fill in the blank spaces in the table.

Change in income	Change in consumption	MPC (marginal propensity to consume)
$2,000	$1,000	
$1,000	$800	
$10,000	$9,500	
$3,456	$2,376	

2. Fill in the blank spaces in the table.

If consumption is	And disposable income is	And the marginal propensity to consume is	Then autonomous consumption is
$400	$1,000	0.20	
$1,600	$1,900	0.80	
$1,700	$2,000	0.75	

3. Fill in the blank spaces in the table.

Consumption	Investment	Net Exports	Total expenditure curve shifts (up, down)
rises	falls by less than consumption rises	rises	
falls	rises by more than consumption falls	falls by more than investment rises	
rises	rises	falls by more than investment rises, but falls by less than consumption rises	

4. Fill in the blank spaces in the table.

MPC	Multiplier
0.75	
0.80	
0.60	

5. Fill in the blank spaces in the table. The consumption function is $C = Co + MPC (Yd)$, where $Co =$ $200 and MPC = 0.80.

Disposable income	Change in disposable income	Consumption	Change in consumption	Saving
$10,000	$0	$8,200	$0	
$12,000				
$14,000				

6. Diagrammatically represent an economy stuck in a recessionary gap (within the AD-AS framework).

Price
Level

└─────────────────────────────────── Real GDP

7. Diagrammatically represent an economy stuck in a recessionary gap (within the TE-TP framework).

TE

└─────────────────────────────────── Real GDP

8. What is the relationship between TE and TP at Q_1? At Q_2? At Q_3?

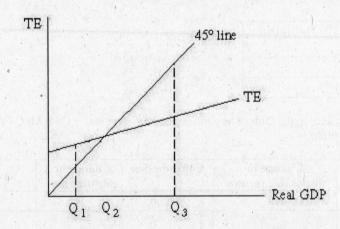

9. Explain what will happen in the economy if it is at Q_1 in the exhibit in question 8.

10. Explain what will happen in the economy if it is at Q_3 in the exhibit in question 8.

What is the Question?
Identify the question for each of the answers that follow.

1. Wages and prices may be inflexible.

2. Autonomous consumption.

3. $1 \div (1 - \text{MPC})$

4. Consumption divided by disposable income.

5. Inventories rise above optimum levels.

What Is Wrong?
In each of the statements that follow, there is something wrong. Identify what is wrong in the space
provided.

1. If the economy is operating on the horizontal section of the Keynesian AS curve, then an increase in
    aggregate demand will raise Real GDP, but a decrease in aggregate demand will lower Real GDP and
    the price level, too.

2. According to Keynes, saving is more responsive to changes in interest rates than to changes in income.

3. Keynes's major work was titled *The General Theory of Employment, Income and Prices,* and it was
    published in 1937.

4. When TE is greater than TP, inventories rise above the optimum inventory level.

5. When the economy is in disequilibrium, inventories are at their optimum levels.

Multiple Choice
Circle the correct answer.

1. If total production is less than total expenditures, then business firms
    a. have underproduced.
    b. will increase production.
    c. have overproduced.
    d. b and c
    e. a and b

2. Consumption is _____ related to disposable income, according to the consumption function discussed in the text..
    a. inversely
    b. directly
    c. inversely at times, directly at other times
    d. not
    e. There is not enough information to answer the question.

3. Less is produced than households want to buy. This holds when
    a. TE = TP.
    b. TP > TE.
    c. TE > TP.
    d. the multiplier is greater than 1.
    e. none of the above

4. The efficiency wage model is an explanation of wage _____ and therefore provides support for _____ economics.
    a. rigidity; classical
    b. flexibility; Keynesian
    c. rigidity; Keynesian
    d. flexibility; classical
    e. flexibility; monetarist

5. Which of the following statements is true?
    a. Keynes believed that monopolistic elements in the economy will prevent immediate price declines.
    b. Keynes believed that during periods of high unemployment, labor unions will prevent wages from falling fast enough to restore full employment.
    c. Keynes believed in Say's law in a barter economy.
    d. all of the above
    e. none of the above

6. Keynes did not believe that interest rate flexibility would ensure that _____ equals saving.
    a. consumption
    b. investment
    c. the multiplier
    d. marginal propensity to consume
    e. net exports

7. Which of the following is an aspect of Keynesian economics?
    a. Wages and prices are flexible.
    b. The economy can exhibit instability.
    c. The private sector can always remove the economy from a recessionary gap.
    d. The economy cannot get stuck in a recessionary gap.
    e. c and d

8. If income rises from $600 to $700 and consumption rises from $300 to $380, the marginal propensity to consume is _____.
   a. 0.54
   b. 0.80
   c. 1.00
   d. 0.65
   e. none of the above

9. If autonomous consumption rises by $600 and as a result real national income rises by $3,000, then the marginal propensity to consume is _____.
   a. 0.90
   b. 0.80
   c. 0.70
   d. 0.60
   e. 0.40

10. According to efficiency wage models,
    a. labor productivity depends on the wage rate the firm pays employees.
    b. labor productivity depends on environmental conditions.
    c. labor specificity is a function of the wage rate.
    d. efficiency is a result of seven production factors.
    e. none of the above

11. In the real world, we should expect the multiplier process to work itself out
    a. almost instantly.
    b. within a few days.
    c. only if the SRAS curve is upward sloping.
    d. only over many months.
    e. c and d

12. In the TE-TP (Keynesian) model, the price level is assumed to be _____, so any changes in TE will bring about a multiplier effect in _____.
    a. rising; consumption
    b. constant; Real GDP
    c. rising; Real GDP
    d. falling; investment
    e. rising; government purchases

13. If investment and government purchases are independent of income, and consumption rises as income rises, then the TE curve will intersect the vertical axis at some point above the origin. The distance between the origin and the point of intersection is equal to
    a. autonomous investment.
    b. autonomous consumption.
    c. autonomous government spending.
    d. net exports.
    e. the multiplier.

14. The ratio of consumption to income is called the
    a. marginal propensity to save.
    b. average propensity to save.
    c. average propensity to consume.
    d. marginal propensity to consume.
    e. There is not enough information to answer the question.

15. If Keynesians believe that the economy can get stuck in a recessionary gap, then they probably don't always hold that _____ is the best policy.
    a. raising consumption
    b. laissez faire
    c. increasing the money supply
    d. a and b
    e. none of the above

True-False
Write a "T" or "F" after each statement.

16. Keynes believed that an increase in saving would not necessarily stimulate an equal amount of added investment spending. ____

17. According to the Keynesian consumption function, consumption spending can be some positive amount even when disposable income is zero. ____

18. When TE > TP, the inventories of firms are rising above their optimum levels. ____

19. According to Keynesians, the economy can be in a recessionary gap and in equilibrium, too. ____

20. According to Keynes, the private sector could not always remove the economy from a recessionary gap. ____

Fill in the Blank
Write the correct word in the blank.

21. _____ _____ models hold that it is sometimes in the best interest of business firms to pay their employees higher-than-equilibrium wage rates.

22. If wages are _____ in the downward direction, it is possible for an economy to get stuck in a recessionary gap.

23. If the economy is operating in the horizontal part of the _____ _____, then any change in aggregate demand will change Real GDP, but not the price level.

24. If the marginal propensity to consume is _____, then the multiplier is 2.5.

25. If people save for a certain dollar goal ($50,000), then it is possible for saving to _____ as interest rates rise.

Chapter 10
Fiscal Policy and the Federal Budget

What This Chapter Is About
In Chapter 8 you learned that some economists believe the economy is self regulating. In Chapter 9, you learned that some economists believe the economy is inherently unstable. If the economy is inherently unstable, if it can't remove itself from recessionary and inflationary gaps, then what is to be done? Some economists propose using fiscal policy to stabilize the economy. Fiscal policy deals with changes in taxes and government expenditures.

Key Concepts in the Chapter
    a. progressive income tax
    b. proportional income tax
    c. regressive income tax
    d. public debt
    e. fiscal policy
    f. crowding out
    g. fiscal policy lags
    h. marginal tax rate
    i. Laffer curve

- **Fiscal policy** deals with changes in government expenditures and/or taxes to achieve particular economic goals, such as low unemployment, stable prices, and economic growth.
- **Crowding out** refers to the decrease in private expenditures that occurs as a consequence of increased government spending or the financing needs of a budget deficit. Crowding out can be complete, incomplete, or zero (no crowding out).
- **Fiscal policy lags** refer to the time it takes to notice and implement certain measures relevant to fiscal policy. There are five fiscal policy lags: data lag, wait-and-see lag, legislative lag, transmission lag, and effectiveness lag.
- The **marginal tax rate** is the ratio of the additional tax paid on the additional income. For example, if one's income rises by $100, and, as a result, one's income tax rises by $35, then the marginal tax rate is 35 percent.
- The **Laffer curve** plots tax revenues against tax rates. It shows that as tax rates initially rise, tax revenues rise, too. However, after some tax rate, further increases in tax rates lower tax revenues.
- A **progressive income tax** refers to an income tax system in which one's tax rate rises as one's taxable income rises (up to some point).
- A **proportional income tax** refers to an income tax system in which one's tax rate is the same no matter what one's taxable income.
- A **regressive income tax** refers to an income tax system in which one's tax rate declines as one's taxable income rises.
- The **public debt** refers to the total amount that the federal government owes its creditors.

Review Questions

1. Give a numerical example that illustrates a progressive income tax structure.

2. Explain why progressive income taxes may not be consistent with after-tax pay for equal work.

3. What is the difference between a cyclical deficit and a structural deficit?

4. What is the difference between automatic and discretionary fiscal policy?

5. What type of fiscal policy would you propose if the economy were in a recessionary gap? Explain your answer.

6. Give an example of incomplete crowding out.

7. If the government spends more on libraries, does it necessarily follow that private spending on books will fall? Explain your answer.

8. Suppose the federal budget is balanced. Then, government spending rises. How might a rise in government spending impact the value of the dollar on foreign currency markets?

9. Suppose that the budget deficit in country A rises. Does it necessarily follow that interest rates will rise? Explain your answer.

10. What is the legislative lag?

11. How can fiscal policy destabilize the economy?

12. Give a numerical example to illustrate the difference between the average tax rate and the marginal tax rate.

13. Will an increase in the average income tax rate bring about greater income tax revenues? Explain your answer.

Problems

Using the following table, answer questions 1-5.

Taxable income	Tax rate
$10,000 – $20,000	10 percent
$20,001 – $30,000	$2,000 + 12 percent of everything over $20,000
$30,001 – $40,000	$3,000 + 14 percent of everything over $30,000

1. If a person earns $15,000, what does she pay in taxes?

2. If a person earns $23,100, what does he pay in taxes?

3. If a person earns $33,988, what does she pay in taxes?

4. What is the marginal tax rate of the person who earns $25,000?

5. What is the marginal tax rate of the person who earns $37,000? What is the person's average tax rate?

6. Fill in the blank spaces in the table.

Total budget deficit	Structural deficit	Cyclical deficit
$250 billion	$100 billion	
$100 billion		$75 billion
	$100 billion	$50 billion

7. There is incomplete crowding out and the economy is in a recessionary gap. Is it possible for
    expansionary fiscal policy to stabilize the economy shown in the diagram? Explain your answer.

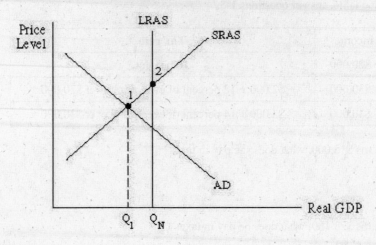

8. Using the diagram that follows, explain how fiscal policy can destabilize the economy.

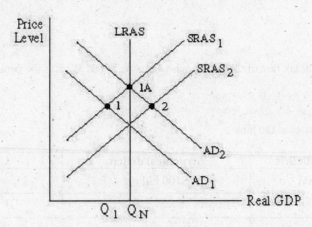

9. Diagrammatically represent the effect on the SRAS and LRAS curves of a permanent marginal tax rate cut.

Price Level

Real GDP

10. Fill in the blank spaces in the table.

Income	Taxes Paid	Marginal tax rate	Average tax rate
$10,000	$2,200	22 percent	22 percent
$11,000	$2,900		
$12,000	$3,700		

11. Fill in the blank spaces in the table.

Taxable income	Tax rate	Tax revenue
$100 million	12.3 percent	
	10.0 percent	$19 million
$200 million		$18 million

What Is the Question?
Identify the question for each of the answers that follow.

1. The same tax rate is used for all income levels.

2. A different tax rate is used for different income levels.

3. It is equal to the total budget deficit minus the cyclical deficit.

4. Changes in government expenditures and/or taxes that occur automatically without (additional) congressional action.

5. Saving increases as a result of the higher future taxes implied by the deficit.

6. The time it takes before policymakers know of a change in the economy.

7. The change in the tax payment divided by the change in taxable income.

8. The downward-sloping part of the Laffer curve.

Multiple Choice
Circle the correct answer.

1. If an economy has a structural deficit and a cyclical deficit, one may conclude that
    a. fiscal policy is contractionary.
    b. fiscal policy is expansionary.
    c. the public debt is rising.
    d. the public debt is falling.
    e. b and c

2. In 2005, federal government spending was what percentage of GDP?
    a. 18.1
    b. 19.9
    c. 19.2
    d. 14.9
    e. 20.1

3. In 2005, federal government tax revenues were what percentage of GDP?
   a. 16.5
   b. 12.4
   c. 19.7
   d. 17.5
   e. 18.4

4. In 2005, the top 1 percent of income earners in the United States paid _____ percent of federal income taxes.
   a. 23.1
   b. 10.2
   c. 33.9
   d. 16.5
   e. 18.6

5. Which of the following is an example of discretionary fiscal policy?
   a. Congress raises taxes.
   b. Congress lowers taxes.
   c. Congress increases spending.
   d. Congress decreases spending.
   e. all of the above

6. Unemployment compensation benefits is an example of
   a. expansionary discretionary fiscal policy.
   b. automatic fiscal policy.
   c. contractionary fiscal policy.
   d. discretionary fiscal policy.
   e. b and d

7. Suppose that the income tax rate rises as taxable income rises. If taxable income rises in the economy, the "higher tax rate at a higher taxable income" is an example of
   a. discretionary fiscal policy.
   b. automatic fiscal policy.
   c. expansionary discretionary fiscal policy.
   d. contractionary discretionary fiscal policy.
   e. There is not enough information to answer the question.

8. Keynesians would propose discretionary contractionary fiscal policy if
   a. the economy was in a recessionary gap.
   b. the economy was in an inflationary gap.
   c. as a stabilizing measure if the economy was in long-run equilibrium.
   d. the economy was stuck below Natural Real GDP.
   e. none of the above

9. Which of the following economists is known for arguing that current taxpayers will likely leave bequests to their heirs for the purpose of paying higher future taxes?
   a. John Maynard Keynes
   b. Robert Barro
   c. Irving Fisher
   d. Robert Solow
   e. Milton Friedman

10. The Laffer curve shows that
    a. as tax rates rise, tax revenues rise.
    b. as tax rates fall, tax revenues fall.
    c. as tax rates fall, tax revenues rise.
    d. as tax rates rise, tax revenues fall.
    e. all of the above

11. Suppose the government attempts to stimulate the economy by increasing purchases without increasing
    taxes. Which of the following statements is most likely to be accepted by someone who believes in
    crowding out?
    a. The government's actions will have their intended effect.
    b. The government's actions will cause businesses to become more optimistic about the economy,
        and they will increase their output even more than the government had intended.
    c. The government's actions will raise interest rates, causing decreased investment and consumption,
        and the economy will not expand as much as the government had intended.
    d. The government's actions will cause households to increase their spending.
    e. none of the above

12. Fiscal policy is likely to be ineffective at removing the economy from a recessionary gap if
    a. there is complete crowding out.
    b. there is zero crowding out.
    c. there are no fiscal policy lags.
    d. the data lag is longer than the legislative lag.
    e. none of the above

13. According to _____ economists, current consumption may fall as a result of _____
    fiscal policy.
    a. Keynesian; discretionary
    b. new classical; expansionary
    c. new classical; contractionary
    d. Keynesian; contractionary
    e. monetarist; contractionary

14. Who said, "High tax rates are followed by attempts of ingenious men to beat them as surely as snow is
    followed by little boys on sleds"?
    a. John Maynard Keynes
    b. Arthur Laffer
    c. Arthur Okun
    d. Robert Barro
    e. none of the above

15. If the percentage decrease in the tax rate is greater than the percentage increase in taxable income, then
    a. the Laffer curve does not hold.
    b. tax revenues will decrease.
    c. tax revenues will increase.
    d. the economy is on the downward-sloping portion of the Laffer curve.
    e. b and d

True-False
Write "T" or "F" after each statement.

16. Fiscal policy can be effective at removing the economy from a recessionary gap. ____

17. If there is complete crowding out, fiscal policy is likely to be ineffective at removing the economy from a recessionary gap. ____

18. New classical economists argue that individuals will link expansionary fiscal policy to higher future taxes and decrease their current consumption and increase saving as a result. ____

19. The effectiveness lag refers to the fact that policymakers are usually not aware of changes in the economy as soon as they happen. ____

20. The change in Real GDP equals the multiplier multiplied by the change in autonomous spending. ____

Fill in the Blank
Write the correct word in the blank.

21. In 2005, the average American worked _____ days to pay all federal, state, and local taxes.

22. The _____ tax rate is equal to the change in one's tax payment divided by the change in one's taxable income.

23. On the _____ - _____ portion of the Laffer curve, a cut in tax rates will raise tax revenue.

24. Tax revenues are equal to the tax base multiplied by the average _____ _____.

25. _____ _____ refers to the decrease in private expenditures that occurs as a consequence of increased government spending and/or the greater financing needs of a budget deficit.

Chapter 11
Money and Banking

What This Chapter Is About
The money supply has not played a role in our discussion of macroeconomics until this point. With this chapter, we begin to talk about money. In fact, this chapter begins a discussion of money that will carry through the rest of our discussion of macroeconomics. In this chapter, we discuss how money came to exist, the money supply, and the money creation process.

Key Concepts in the Chapter
    a. money
    b. barter
    c. fractional reserve banking

- **Money** is any good that is widely accepted for purposes of exchange in the repayment of debts.
- **Barter** refers to exchanging goods and services for other goods and services without the use of money.
- **Fractional reserve banking** is a banking arrangement that allows banks to hold reserves equal to only a fraction of their deposit liabilities.

Review Questions

1. Give an example of two people who have a double coincidence of wants.

2. What does it mean to say that money is a unit of account?

3. Explain the part that self interest plays in the story of money emerging from a barter economy.

4.   The use of money makes the consumption of additional leisure possible. Explain.

5.   What gives money value?

6.   What does the M1 money supply equal?

7.   What does the M2 money supply equal?

8.   Since credit cards are widely accepted for purposes of exchange, why aren't they considered money?

9.   What do a bank's reserves consist of?

10. If checkable deposits in Bank A go from $400 million to $450 million, will Bank A have to hold more reserves? Explain your answer.

11. Give an example of a cash leakage.

12. What is the difference between the required-reserve ratio and the simple deposit multiplier?

Problems

1. Fill in the blanks in the table.

Required-reserve ratio	Simple deposit multiplier
0.10	
0.12	
0.09	

2. Fill in the blanks in the table.

Currency	Checkable deposits	Traveler's checks	M1 money supply
$200 billion	$500 billion	$8 billion	
$100 billion		$9 billion	$700 billion
	$300 billion	$10 billion	$500 billion

3. Fill in the blanks in the table.

Checkable deposits	Required-reserve ratio	Required reserves
$400 million	0.10	
$300 million	0.12	
$1,000 million	0.15	

4. Fill in the blanks in the table.

Checkable deposits	Required-reserve ratio	Required reserves	Reserves	Excess reserves
$400 million	0.10		$60 million	
$500 million	0.15		$80 million	
$872 million	0.12		$200 million	

5. Fill in the blanks in the table.

Checkable deposits	Required-reserve ratio	Required reserves	Vault cash	Bank deposits at the Fed	Excess reserves
$230 million	0.13		$10 million	$30 million	
$367 million	0.10		$1 million	$43 million	
$657 million	0.12		$23 million	$60 million	

6. Fill in the blanks in the table.

Change in reserves	Required-reserve ratio	Maximum change in the money supply
+ $4 million	0.10	
+ $50 million	0.12	
- $41 million	0.10	

7. Fill in the blanks in the table.

Checkable deposits	Required-reserve ratio	Required reserves	Vault cash	Bank deposits at the Fed	Excess reserves
$1,000 million	0.10		$50 million		$0
$230 million	0.12		$20 million		$0
$498 million	0.10		$10 million		$0

What Is the Question?
Identify the question for each of the answers that follow.

1. Medium of exchange, unit of account, and store of value.

2. Exchanging goods and services for other goods and services.

3. The least exclusive function of money.

4. General acceptability.

5. Deposits on which checks can be written.

6. An asset that can easily and quickly be turned into cash.

7. The central bank of the United States.

8. Bank deposits at the Fed plus vault cash.

9. The difference between reserves and required reserves.

10. 1 divided by the required-reserve ratio.

What Is Wrong?
In each of the statements that follow, something is wrong. Identify what is wrong in the space provided.

1. How much money did you earn last week?

2. A double coincidence of wants is not a necessary condition for trade to take place.

3. The largest component of M1 is currency.

4. M1 is the broad definition of the money supply.

5. Excess reserves equal reserves plus required reserves.

6. The maximum change in checkable deposits = r x ΔR.

7. The greater the cash leakages, the larger the increase in the money supply for a given positive change in reserves.

8. Our money today has value because it is backed by gold.

Multiple Choice
Circle the correct answer.

1. If chalk is widely accepted for purposes of exchange, then
    a.   chalk is money.
    b.   chalk is less valuable than it was before it was widely accepted for purposes of exchange.
    c.   we would observe people using chalk to buy their weekly groceries.
    d.   a and b
    e.   a and c

2. Money is valuable because
    a.   it is backed by gold.
    b.   the government says it is valuable.
    c.   people are willing to accept it in payment for goods and services.
    d.   it is backed by silver.
    e.   none of the above

3. A common measurement in which values are expressed is referred to as a
    a.   medium of exchange.
    b.   store of value.
    c.   unit of account.
    d.   barter payment.
    e.   none of the above

4. M1 is comprised of
    a.   currency, checkable deposits, Visa and MasterCard.
    b.   currency, checkable deposits, traveler's checks.
    c.   currency and checkable deposits.
    d.   currency, checkable deposits, savings deposits.

5. A credit card is
    a.   considered money.
    b.   not considered money.
    c.   under certain circumstances considered money.
    d.   the same as a repurchase agreement.
    e.   none of the above

6. Reserves equal
    a.   demand deposits + vault cast – traveler's checks.
    b.   currency + savings deposits – vault cash.
    c.   bank deposits at the Fed + vault cash + currency.
    d.   bank deposits at the Fed + vault cash.

7. If deposits in Bank A total $15 million and the required-reserve ratio is 10 percent, then excess reserves equal _____.
    a. $13.5 million.
    b. $1.5 million.
    c. $10.5 million.
    d. $2.5 million.
    e. none of the above

8. Which of the following required-reserve rations would allow a bank the least amount of loanable funds?
    a. 5 percent
    b. 10 percent
    c. 12 percent
    d. 15 percent

9. The banking system increases the money supply by
    a. printing its own currency.
    b. creating checkable deposits.
    c. creating demand deposits and currency.
    d. creating Federal Reserve Notes.
    e. none of the above

10. Suppose that the excess reserves in Bank A increase by $3,000. If the required-reserve ratio is 20 percent, what is the maximum change in demand deposits brought about by the banking system?
    a. $15,000
    b. $12,000
    c. $10,000
    d. $8,500
    e. none of the above

11. Which of the following statements is false?
    a. A change in the composition of the money supply always decreases the money supply.
    b. If Smith takes $1,000 out of her wallet and deposits it in a bank, the composition of the money supply changes.
    c. If Jones takes $1,000 out of his checking account in the bank and puts it in his wallet, the composition of the money supply changes.
    d. A change in the composition of the money supply can change the size of the money supply.
    e. a and c

12. The simple deposit multiplier is
    a. the required-reserve ratio.
    b. always 1.
    c. the reciprocal of the required-reserve ratio.
    d. different from bank to bank even if the required-reserve ratio is the same for all banks.

13. If there is a change in the composition of the money supply such that there is more currency outside banks and less checkable deposits, the money supply
    a. falls.
    b. rises.
    c. stays constant.
    d. first falls and then sharply rises.

14. If the required-reserve ratio is 20 percent, the simple deposit multiplier is _____.
    a. 3
    b. 4
    c. 5
    d. 6
    e. none of the above

15. Bank A has deposits of $10,000 and reserves of $3,600. If the required-reserve ratio is 0.20 (20%), the bank has excess reserves of _____.
    a. $2,000
    b. $3,600
    c. $1,200
    d. $1,600
    e. none of the above

True-False
Write a "T" or "F" after each statement.

16. A unit of account is a common measurement in which values are expressed. ____

17. Money is unique in that it is the only good that serves as a store of value. ____

18. Money market mutual funds invest in short-term, highly illiquid assets. ____

19. The more new reserves that enter the banking system, the greater the money supply will be, *ceteris paribus.* ____

20. Money did not exist before formal governments existed. ____

Fill in the Blank
Write the correct word in the blank.

21. Two people have a _____ _____ ____ _____ if what the first person wants is what the second person has, and what the second person wants is what the first person has.

22. _____ equal bank deposits at the Fed plus vault cash.

23. Under a _____ _____ banking system, banks create money by holding on reserve only a fraction of the money deposited with them and lending the remainder.

24. If the required-reserve ratio is 10 percent, the simple deposit multiplier is _____.

25. Money has value because of its _____ _____.

Chapter 12
The Federal Reserve System

What This Chapter Is About
The last chapter briefly mentioned the Federal Reserve System. In this chapter the Fed is discussed at some length. A brief history of the Fed is presented, the functions of the Fed discussed, and the tools the Fed uses to change the money supply are explained.

Key Concepts in the Chapter
    a.   open market operations
    b.   federal funds rate
    c.   discount rate

- **Open market operations** refer to the buying and selling of government securities by the Fed. When the Fed buys government securities, it is conducting an open market purchase; when it sells government securities, it is conducting an open market sale.
- The **federal funds rate** is the interest rate one bank charges another to borrow reserves. Stated differently, it is the interest rate one bank charges another for a loan.
- The **discount rate** is the interest rate the Fed charges depository institutions that borrow reserves from it. Stated differently, it is the interest rate the Fed charges depository institutions for a loan.

Review Questions

1. How many people sit on the Board of Governors of the Federal Reserve System?

2. How many Federal Reserve districts exist?

3. Identify the locations of the Federal Reserve District Banks.

4. What is the most important responsibility of the Fed?

5.   What is the composition of the Federal Open Market Committee (FOMC)?

6.   Explain how a check is cleared.

7.   What is the difference between the Treasury and the Fed?

8.   Explain how an open market purchase increases the money supply.

9.   Explain how lowering the discount rate (relative to the funds rate) increases the money supply.

10. Give a numerical example that shows how lowering the required-reserve ratio can increase the money supply.

11. Is the federal funds rate determined in a different way than the discount rate? Explain your answer.

Problems

1. Here are some data for Bank A:
    Checkable deposits = $400 million
    Required-reserve ratio = 10 percent
    Required reserves = $40 million
    Reserves = $40 million
    Excess reserves = 0

    Suppose now the required-reserve ratio is lowered to 5 percent. What do the following equal?

    Checkable deposits = _____ million
    Required-reserve ratio = _____ percent
    Required reserves = _____ million
    Reserves = _____ million
    Excess reserves = _____ million

2. Here are some data for Bank B:
    Checkable deposits = $500 million
    Required-reserve ratio = 12 percent
    Required reserves = $60 million
    Reserves = $60 million
    Excess reserves = 0

    Suppose now the Fed buys $10 million worth of securities from Bank B. What do the following equal?

    Checkable deposits = _____ million
    Required-reserve ratio = _____ percent
    Required reserves = _____ million
    Reserves = _____ million
    Excess reserves = _____ million

3. Here are some data for Bank C:
    Checkable deposits = $600 million
    Required-reserve ratio = 10 percent
    Required reserves = $60 million
    Reserves = $60 million
    Excess reserves = 0

    Suppose now Fed buys $10 million worth of securities from Jane, who does her banking at Bank C.
    The Fed writes a check to Jane for $10 million. Jane deposits the entire check in her account with Bank
    C. What do the following equal?

    Checkable deposits = _____ million
    Required-reserve ratio = _____ percent
    Required reserves = _____ million
    Reserves = _____ million
    Excess reserves = _____ million

4. Here are some data for Bank D:
       Checkable deposits = $600 million
       Required-reserve ratio = 10 percent
       Required reserves = $60 million
       Reserves = $60 million
       Excess reserves = 0

Suppose now that the Fed gives a $10 million discount loan to Bank D. What do the following equal?

       Checkable deposits = _____ million
       Required-reserve ratio = _____ percent
       Required reserves = _____ million
       Reserves = _____ million
       Excess reserves = _____ million

5. Fill in the blanks in the table.

Fed action...	Money supply (rises, falls, remains unchanged)
Conducts an open market purchase	
Lowers required-reserve ratio	
Raises the discount rate to a level higher than the federal funds rate	
Conducts an open market sale	
Lowers the discount rate to a level substantially lower than the federal funds rate	
Raises the required-reserve ratio	

6. Fill in the blanks in the table. Assume that the required-reserve ratio is 10 percent.

Fed action...	Maximum change in the money supply
Buys $100 million worth of government securities from Bank A	
Gives a $10 million discount loan to Bank B	
Sells $20 million worth of government securities to Bank C	

What Is the Question?
Identify the question for each of the answers that follow.

1. Any of these changes in Fed policy tools will cause the money supply to rise.

2. This group conducts open market operations.

3. These are sold to raise funds to pay the government's bills.

4. The Fed buys and sells government securities.

5. Either to the federal funds market or to the Fed for a discount loan.

What Is Wrong?
In each of the statements that follow, something is wrong. Identify what is wrong in the space provided.

1. The president of the St. Louis Fed holds a permanent seat on the FOMC.

2. The Fed is a budgetary and monetary agency and the Treasury is a budgetary agency only.

3. An open market purchase refers to a commercial bank buying government securities from the Fed.

4. An increase in the discount rate is likely to raise the money supply.

5.   The major responsibility of the Fed is to clear checks.

Multiple Choice
Circle the correct answer.

1.   _____ persons sit on the FOMC.
     a.   12
     b.   7
     c.   15
     d.   10
     e.   13

2.   When a check is written on an account at Bank C and is deposited in Bank D, the reserve account of _____ will fall while reserves of the entire banking system _____.
     a.   Bank C; rise
     b.   Bank C; remain unchanged
     c.   Bank D; rise
     d.   Bank D; remain unchanged

3.   Suppose the public begins to withdraw a lot of currency from the banking system. The Fed could offset the effect on the money supply by
     a.   buying government securities.
     b.   raising the required-reserve ratio.
     c.   raising the discount rate.
     d.   selling government securities.
     e.   none of the above

4.   A bank is less likely to borrow reserves from the Fed when the _____ rises relative to the _____.
     a.   discount rate; required-reserve ratio
     b.   federal funds rate; discount rate
     c.   required-reserve ratio; discount rate
     d.   discount rate; federal funds rate
     e.   federal funds rate; required-reserve ratio

5.   An open market purchase occurs when
     a.   one bank buys government securities from another bank.
     b.   a bank buys government securities from the Fed.
     c.   the Fed buys government securities from a bank.
     d.   the Fed raises the discount rate.
     e.   none of the above

6.   The Fed
     a.   serves as a fiscal agent for the Treasury.
     b.   is a lender of last resort.
     c.   is a borrower of last resort.
     d.   a and b
     e.   a, b, and c

7. The Fed began operation in
   a. 1913.
   b. 1914.
   c. 1915.
   d. 1929.
   e. none of the above

8. If the Fed purchases government securities from a commercial bank, which of the following will happen?
   a. The Fed will increase the bank's reserves on deposit at the Fed.
   b. The Fed will decrease the bank's reserves on deposit at the Fed.
   c. The assets (government securities) of the Fed will decrease.
   d. The assets (government securities) of the Fed will increase.
   e. a and d

9. The Fed considers the ability of a bank to borrow from it a(n)
   a. honor.
   b. right.
   c. virtue.
   d. privilege.

10. In the federal funds market,
    a. banks make loans to the Fed.
    b. banks make loans to other banks.
    c. the Fed makes short-term loans to banks.
    d. the Fed makes long-term loans to banks.

True-False
Write "T" or "F" after each statement.

11. Open market sales reduce the money supply. ____

12. The Federal Open Market Committee is composed of the members of the Board of Governors, among others. ____

13. Open market purchases increase the money supply. ____

14. A decline in the required-reserve ratio will lower the money supply. ____

15. A fall in the discount rate (relative to the federal funds rate) will lower the money supply. ____

Fill in the Blank
Write the correct word in the blank.

16. A(an) _____ in the discount rate will lower the money supply and a (an) _____ in the required-reserve ratio will raise the money supply.

17. The interest rate that one bank charges another bank is called the _____ _____ _____.

18. The president of the Federal Reserve Bank of _____ is always a member of the FOMC.

19. A(n) _____ _____ _____ occurs when the Fed buys government securities from a bank.

20. If one bank borrows funds from another bank, the money supply will _____ _____.

Chapter 13
Money and the Economy

What This Chapter Is About
Earlier chapters discussed a few of the technical details of money—how money came to exist, what the money supply is, how the money supply is increased and decreased. This chapter deals with how money affects the economy.

Key Concepts in the Chapter
   a. equation of exchange
   b. simple quantity theory of money
   c. one-shot inflation
   d. continued inflation
   e. deflation
   f. velocity

- The **equation of exchange** is an identify stating that the money supply multiplied by velocity is equal to the price level multiplied by Real GDP.
- The **simple quantity theory of money** predicts that changes in the price level are strictly proportional to changes in the money supply.
- **One-shot inflation** is a one-time increase in the money supply.
- **Continued inflation** is a continued, or sustained, increase in the money supply.
- **Deflation** is a decrease in the price level.
- **Velocity** is the average number of times a dollar is spent to buy final goods and services in a year.

Review Questions

1. Give an example to illustrate velocity.

2. What is the difference between the equation of exchange and the simple quantity theory of money?

3. What does the simple quantity theory of money predict?

4. What does the aggregate supply curve look like in the simple quantity theory of money? Explain your answer.

5. Use the equation of exchange to explain inflation and deflation.

6. What is the monetarist position on the following:

    a. the shape of the SRAS curve

    b. the factors that change AD in the economy

    c. velocity

    d. the issue of a self-regulating economy

7. One-shot inflation can be caused by a change in a factor on the demand-side of the economy or on the supply-side of the economy. Do you agree or disagree? Explain your answer.

8. Is continued inflation a demand-side (of the economy) or supply-side phenomenon? Explain your answer.

9. What is the liquidity effect?

10. What is the expectations, or Fisher, effect?

11. Explain how a change in the money supply can affect the interest rate.

12. What is the difference between the nominal interest rate and the real interest rate?

Problems

1. Fill in the blanks in the table. Assume that velocity and Real GDP are constant.

Percentage change in the money supply	Percentage change in the price level
+ 25	
− 10	
+ 9	

2. Fill in the blanks in the table.

Money supply	Velocity	Real GDP	Will there be inflation or deflation?
rises	rises	stays constant	
falls	stays constant	rises	
falls	falls	rises	

3. The economy is initially in long-run equilibrium. Then, the money supply rises. According to monetarists, what will happen to the price level and to Real GDP in the short run and in the long run?

4. The economy is initially in long-run equilibrium. Then, velocity falls. According to monetarists, what will happen to the price level and to Real GDP in the short run and in the long run?

5. The economy is initially in long-run equilibrium. Diagrammatically represent one-shot inflation that is demand induced.

Price
Level
|
|
|
|
|
|
|
|
|_____ Real GDP

6. The economy is initially in long-run equilibrium. Diagrammatically represent one-shot inflation that is supply induced.

Price
Level
|
|
|
|
|
|
|
|
|_____ Real GDP

7. What would you see in the world if continued inflation were supply induced? Explain your answer.

8. Diagrammatically represent the liquidity effect. Assume the money supply falls.

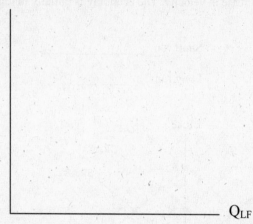

9. Diagrammatically represent the expectations effect. Assume the money supply rises.

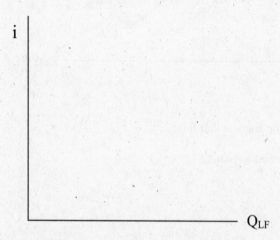

10. Using the figure, identify the route a monetarist would predict the economy would take in the short run and in the long run due to an increase in the money supply. The economy is initially in long-run equilibrium, at point A.

Short run: _____

Long run: _____

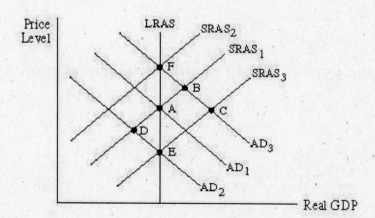

11. Using the figure, identify the route a monetarist would predict the economy would take in the short run and in the long run due to a decrease in velocity. The economy is initially in long-run equilibrium, at point A.

Short run: _____

Long run: _____

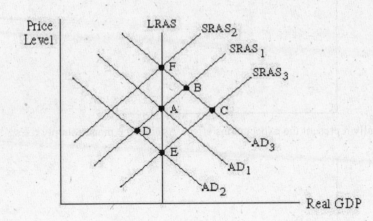

What Is the Question?
Identify the question for each of the answers that follow.

1. In the theory, velocity is assumed constant.

2. In the theory, the AS curve is vertical.

3. This can happen if the money supply rises, velocity rises, or if Real GDP falls.

4. According to these economists, changes in velocity can change aggregate demand.

5. The change in the interest rate due to a change in the expected inflation rate.

6. The change in the interest rate due to a change in the price level.

7. The real interest rate plus the expected inflation rate.

What Is Wrong?
In each of the statements that follow, something is wrong. Identify what is wrong in the space provided.

1. An increase in velocity and a decrease in Real GDP will lead to a decline in the price level.

2. In both the simple quantity theory of money and the monetarist theory, the aggregate demand curve will shift right or left if either the money supply or interest rates change.

3. According to monetarists, prices are flexible but wages are inflexible.

4. The CPI rises from 100 to 120, to 130, to 135, to 145, and so on. This is indicative of one-shot inflation.

5. Continued decreases in short-run aggregate supply can lead to continued deflation.

Multiple Choice
Circle the correct answer.

1. The velocity of money can be expressed as
    a. GDP/M.
    b. PQ/M.
    c. M x P/GDP.
    d. Q/M.
    e. a and b

2. The money supply is $700 billion, velocity is 2, and Real GDP is 300 units of goods and services. According to the simple quantity theory of money, if the money supply rises to $800, the average price in the economy will rise to _____.
    a. $4.25
    b. $5.33
    c. $10.00
    d. $2.50
    e. There is not enough information to answer the question.

3. According to the simple quantity theory of money, which of the following will lead to a change in aggregate demand?
    a. a change in velocity
    b. a change in wage rates
    c. a change in interest rates
    d. a change in the money supply
    e. a and d

4. According to monetarists, which of the following will lead to a change in aggregate demand?
    a. a change in velocity
    b. a change in wage rates
    c. a change in interest rates
    d. a change in the money supply
    e. a and d

5. Which of the following describes the monetarist view of the economy?
    a. The economy is self regulating, wages are rigid, and velocity is unpredictable.
    b. The economy is self regulating, wages are flexible, prices are flexible.
    c. Velocity changes in a predictable way.
    d. The SRAS curve is vertical at the existing Real GDP level.
    e. b and c

6. Monetarists believe that changes in velocity and the money supply will change _____ in the short run, but only _____ in the long run.
    a. the price level and Real GDP; Real GDP
    b. interest rates and Real GDP; the price level
    c. the price level and Real GDP; the price level
    d. only interest rates; the price level
    e. none of the above

7. Which of the following will lead to one-shot inflation?
   a. continued increases in the money supply
   b. continued decreases in SRAS
   c. continued increases in the nominal interest rate
   d. b and c
   e. none of the above

8. Which of the following can turn one-shot inflation into continued inflation?
   a. continued increases in long-run aggregate supply
   b. continued decreases in real interest rates
   c. continued increases in aggregate demand
   d. continued increases in short-run aggregate supply
   e. c and d

9. The change in the interest rate brought on by a change in Real GDP is referred to as the
   a. liquidity effect.
   b. income effect.
   c. price-level effect.
   d. expectations effect.
   e. Fisher effect.

10. If the simple quantity theory of money predicts well, what would we expect to see (in the real world)?
    a. changes in the money supply strongly correlated with changes in interest rates
    b. changes in the money supply strongly correlated with changes in inflation rates
    c. changes in Real GDP strongly correlated with changes in the money supply
    d. changes in velocity strongly correlated with changes in the money supply
    e. none of the above

11. The economy is initially in long-run equilibrium. The short-run aggregate supply (SRAS) curve shifts to the left. As the result, there is _____. Assuming the economy is self-regulating, the price level will soon _____, unless either the _____ curve shifts to the left or the _____ curve shifts to the _____.
    a. one-shot inflation; rise; SRAS; AD; left
    b. continued inflation; fall; SRAS; AD; right
    c. one-shot inflation; rise; AD; SRAS; right
    d. one-shot inflation; fall; SRAS; AD; right
    e. none of the above

12. According to Milton Friedman, continued inflation is always and everywhere
    a. a supply-side phenomenon.
    b. caused by continued decreases in aggregate supply.
    c. caused by continued increases in the budget deficit.
    d. a monetary phenomenon.
    e. none of the above

13. Wages begin to rise, the SRAS curve shifts to the left, and the price level rises. Under what condition(s) is the increase in the price level (one-shot inflation) demand induced?
    a. Under no condition.
    b. Under the conditions that the economy was initially in long-run equilibrium, that it is self-regulating, and that the AD curve initially shifted to the right.
    c. Under the conditions that the economy was initially in long-run equilibrium, that it is self-regulating, and that the AD curve initially shifted to the left.
    d. Under the conditions that the economy was initially in long-run equilibrium, that it is not self-regulating, and that the AD curve shifted neither to the right nor to the left.

14. If GDP is $8,420 billion and the money supply is $1,010 billion, velocity is _____.
   a. 2.21
   b. 4.19
   c. 4.31
   d. 6.31
   e. none of the above

True-False
Write a "T" or "F" after each statement.

15. An increase in velocity and an increase in the money supply will shift the AD curve to the left. ____

16. Total spending or expenditures (measured by MV) must equal the total sales revenues of business firms (measured by PV). ____

17. The monetarist theory of the economy holds that velocity is constant and Real GDP rises by a small percentage on an annual basis. ____

18. The California gold rush led to a decrease in the amount of money in circulation. ____

19. A decrease in the money supply and a decrease in velocity will cause the price level to fall, *ceteris paribus*. ____

Fill in the Blank
Write the correct word in the blank.

20. The AD curve shifts rightward and the price level rises. This is an example of _____ – _____ inflation.

21. The SRAS curve shifts leftward and the price level rises. This is an example of _____ – _____ inflation.

22. The _____ _____ is the only factor that can continually increase without causing a reduction in one of the four components of total expenditures.

23. A change in the expected inflation rate affects both the _____ _____ and _____ _____ loanable funds.

24. The _____ _____ _____ is equal to the nominal interest rate minus the expected inflation rate.

Chapter 14
Monetary Policy

What This Chapter Is About
There are two types of economic policy the government can use to affect the economy. One is fiscal policy, the other is monetary policy. Fiscal policy was discussed in an earlier chapter. In this chapter, monetary policy is discussed.

Key Concepts in the Chapter
    a.   monetary policy
    b.   transmission mechanism
    c.   fine-tuning

- **Monetary policy** deals with changes in the money supply or with changes in the rate of growth of the money supply.
- The **transmission mechanism** refers to the routes or channels that ripple effects created in the money market travel to affect the goods and services market.
- **Fine-tuning** refers to the usually frequent use of monetary and fiscal policies to counteract even small undesirable movements in economic activity.

Review Questions

1. What does the demand for money have to do with the opportunity cost of holding money?

2. Explain how the Keynesian transmission mechanism works.

3. How does the money market equilibrate? In short, what happens if there is either a surplus or shortage of money?

4. What does it mean if investment is interest insensitive? How will interest-insensitive investment affect the Keynesian transmission mechanism?

5. Explain why bond prices and interest rates move in opposite directions.

6. Explain how the monetarist transmission mechanism works.

7. What is expansionary monetary policy? What is contractionary monetary policy?

8. Explain how expansionary monetary policy is supposed to remove an economy from a recessionary gap.

9. Explain how contractionary monetary policy is supposed to remove an economy from a contractionary gap.

10. What are the three points activists make as to why activist monetary policy is preferred to a monetary rule?

11. Use the exhibit to explain how expansionary monetary policy can destabilize the economy.

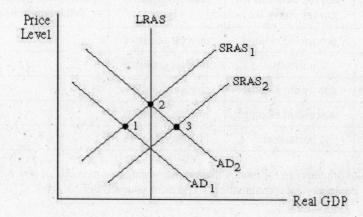

Problems

1. Assume the Keynesian transmission mechanism is operational and the economy is operating in the horizontal part of the Keynesian AS curve. Fill in the blank spaces in the table.

If the money supply…	And the demand for money curve is…	And investment is…	Then Real GDP will (rise, fall, remain unchanged)
rises	downward sloping	interest sensitive	
falls	horizontal	interest sensitive	
rises	downward sloping	interest insensitive	
falls	downward sloping	interest sensitive	
rises	horizontal	interest sensitive	

2. Assume the Monetarist transmission mechanism is operational. Fill in the blank spaces in the table.

If the money supply…	And the demand for money curve is…	And investment is…	Then Real GDP will (rise, fall, remain unchanged)
rises	downward sloping	interest sensitive	
falls	downward sloping	interest sensitive	
rises	downward sloping	interest insensitive	
falls	downward sloping	interest insensitive	

3. Assume the Keynesian transmission mechanism is operational and that the aggregate supply curve is horizontal. Fill in the blanks in the table.

If the money supply…	And the demand for money curve is…	And investment is…	Then the price level will (rise, fall, remain unchanged)
rises	downward sloping	interest sensitive	
falls	horizontal	interest sensitive	
rises	downward sloping	interest insensitive	
falls	downward sloping	interest sensitive	
rises	horizontal	interest sensitive	

4. There is a surplus of money in the money market. According to a monetarist, how will this affect the goods and services market? Diagrammatically represent your answer.

Price
Level

Real GDP

5. There is a surplus of money in the money market. Also, investment is sensitive to changes in interest rates. According to a Keynesian, how will this affect the goods and services market? (Assume the economy is operating in the horizontal section of the AS curve.) Diagrammatically represent your answer.

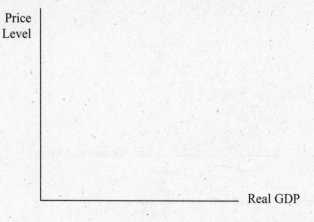

6. The economy is self regulating and in a recessionary gap. If expansionary monetary policy is used to remove the economy from a recessionary gap, will the price level end up higher or lower than it would have had nothing been done?

7. The economy is self regulating and in an inflationary gap. If contractionary monetary policy is used to remove the economy from an inflationary gap, will the price level end up higher or lower than it would have had nothing been done?

8. The objective is to keep prices stable. Fill in the blank spaces in the table.

Percentage change in velocity	Percentage change in Real GDP	Percentage change in the money supply
+ 2 percent	+ 3 percent	
− 1 percent	+ 2 percent	
+ 2 percent	− 3 percent	

9. Diagrammatically represent a liquidity trap.

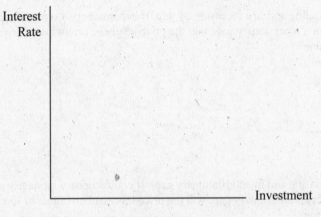

10. Diagrammatically represent interest-insensitive investment.

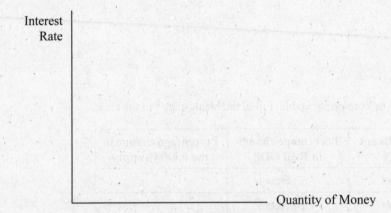

11. Diagrammatically represent a surplus in the money market.

Interest
Rate

Quantity of Money

12. Diagrammatically represent how expansionary monetary policy ideally works if the economy is in a recessionary gap.

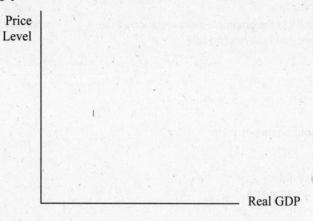

What Is the Question?
Identify the question for each of the answers that follow.

1. The money supply rises but the interest rate does not fall.

2. The interest rate falls, but investment does not increase.

3. A change in the money supply directly leads to a change in aggregate demand.

4. Activist monetary policy may not work, activist monetary policy may be destabilizing, and wages and prices are sufficiently flexible to allow the economy to equilibrate at reasonable speed at Natural Real GDP.

5. If velocity rises by 2 percent, and Real GDP rises by 3 percent, then increase the money supply by 1 percent.

6. The federal funds rate target = inflation (or current inflation rate) + equilibrium real federal funds rate + 1/2 (inflation gap) + 1/2 (output gap).

Multiple Choice
Circle the correct answer.

1. The demand curve for money is the graphical representation of the _____ relationship between the quantity demanded of money and the interest rate.
    a.   direct
    b.   rising
    c.   constant
    d.   inverse

2. The opportunity cost of holding money is the
    a.   interest rate.
    b.   price of gold.
    c.   inverse of the price of gold.
    d.   inverse of the interest rate minus 1.

3. Equilibrium in the money market occurs when the
    a.   quantity demanded of money equals the quantity wanted of money.
    b.   quantity demanded of money equals the quantity supplied of money divided by the appropriate interest rate.
    c.   quantity supplied of money equals the quantity demanded of money.
    d.   b or c
    e.   none of the above

4. As the interest rate rises, the quantity demanded of money
    a.   rises.
    b.   falls.
    c.   usually does not change.
    d.   There is not enough information to answer the question.

5. Which scenario best explains the Keynesian transmission mechanism if the money market is in the liquidity trap?
    a.   The money market is initially in equilibrium; the money supply rises; there is an excess demand for money; the interest rate rises; investment falls.
    b.   The money market is initially in equilibrium; the money supply rises; there is an excess supply of money that puts downward pressure on interest rates; investment rises.
    c.   The money market is initially in equilibrium; the money supply rises; there is an excess supply of money that puts downward pressure on interest rates; investment is unresponsive to the lower interest rate.
    d.   The money market is initially in equilibrium; the money supply rises; there is no excess supply of money; the interest rate does not drop; investment does not change.

6. Suppose the price of old and existing bonds are falling. This means that you can expect to see market interest rates
    a.   on the decline.
    b.   on the rise.
    c.   first going up and then coming down.
    d.   first coming down and then going up.

7. Compared to the Keynesian transmission mechanism, the monetarist transmission mechanism is
    a.   indirect and long.
    b.   direct and long.
    c.   direct and short.
    d.   indirect and short.

8. Which of the following statements is false?
   a. In the monetarist transmission mechanism, changes in the money market only indirectly affect aggregate demand.
   b. In the monetarist transmission mechanism, there is need for the money market to affect the loanable funds market or the investment market before aggregate demand is affected.
   c. In the monetarist transmission mechanism, if individuals are faced with an excess supply of money they spend that money on a wide variety of goods.
   d. a and b
   e. a, b, and c

9. Keynesians would not be likely to advocate expansionary monetary policy to eliminate a recessionary gap if they believed
   a. the liquidity trap exists.
   b. investment spending is interest sensitive.
   c. monetarists were in favor of such a policy.
   d. a and b
   e. a, b, and c

10. Read the following statements:
    (1) The more closely monetary policy can be designed to meet the particulars of a given economic environment, the better.
    (2) Because of long and uncertain time lags, activist monetary policy may be destabilizing rather than stabilizing.
    (3) There is sufficient flexibility in wages and prices in modern economies to allow the economy to equilibrate in reasonable speed at the natural level of Real GNP.
    (4) The "same-for-all-seasons" monetary policy is the way to proceed.

    Which of the statements is likely to be made by an economist who believes in activist monetary policy?
    a. statements 1, 2, and 3
    b. statements 1 and 4
    c. statements 1 and 3
    d. statement 1
    e. statements 1, 3, and 4

11. An economist who proposes a money growth rule (and assumes velocity does not change) will often argue that setting the annual growth rate in the money supply equal to the average annual growth rate in Real GDP
    a. maintains price level stability over time.
    b. is a way to raise investment.
    c. will cause the price level to fall over time and interest rates to stabilize.
    d. a and b
    e. a, b, and c

12. The quantity demanded of money rises as the
    a. interest rate rises.
    b. interest rate falls.
    c. supply of money falls.
    d. none of the above, since the quantity demanded of money is unrelated to the interest rate

13. What does it mean if the investment demand curve is completely insensitive to changes in interest rates?
    a. Changes in the interest rates will lower but not raise investment spending.
    b. Changes in the interest rates will raise but not lower investment spending.
    c. Changes in the interest rates will not change investment spending.
    d. Changes in the interest rates within a certain range will not change investment spending.

14. When is it best to buy bonds?
    a. When interest rates are expected to rise, because this means bond prices will rise.
    b. When interest rates are expected to fall, because this means bond prices will fall.
    c. When interest rates are expected to rise, because this means bond prices will fall.
    d. When interest rates are expected to fall, because this means bond prices will rise.

True-False
Write a "T" or "F" after each statement.

15. Most Keynesians believe that the natural forces of the market economy work much more quickly and assuredly at eliminating an inflationary gap than a recessionary gap. ____

16. The price of old or existing bonds is directly related to the market interest rate. ____

17. Activists are less likely to advocate fine-tuning the economy than nonactivists. ____

18. The demand curve for money is usually vertical. ____

19. It has been argued that Keynesian monetary policy has a deflationary bias to it. ____

Fill in the Blank
Write the correct word in the blank.

20. Keynesians would not likely propose expansionary monetary policy to cure a recessionary gap if investment was interest _____ or the money market was in the _____ _____.

21. In the monetarist transmission mechanism, changes in the money market _____ affect aggregate demand.

22. Keynesians are less likely to propose _____ monetary policy to eliminate an inflationary gap than _____ monetary policy to eliminate a recessionary gap.

23. The Taylor Rule specifies that the federal funds rate target equals inflation (current inflation rate) plus the _____ _____ _____ _____ _____ plus 1/2 (inflation gap) plus 1/2 (output gap).

24. _____ _____ requires that the Fed try to keep the inflation rate near a predetermined level.

Chapter 15
Expectations Theory and the Economy

What This Chapter Is About

Until this chapter, expectations have been absent from the story of macroeconomics. In this chapter, they occupy center stage. Two expectations theories are discussed in this chapter—adaptive and rational. Often, peoples' expectations can influence macroeconomic outcomes.

Key Concepts in the Chapter
    a.   Phillips curve
    b.   adaptive expectations
    c.   rational expectations
    d.   policy ineffectiveness proposition

- The **Phillips curve** shows the historical relationship between price inflation and unemployment.
- **Adaptive expectations** are expectations that individuals form based on past experience.
- **Rational expectations** are expectations that individuals form based on past experience and also on their predictions about the effects of present and future policy actions and events.
- According to the **policy ineffectiveness proposition** (PIP), if (1) a policy change is correctly anticipated, (2) individuals form their expectations rationally, and (3) wages and prices are flexible, then neither fiscal policy nor monetary policy is effective at meeting macroeconomic goals.

Review Questions

1.   What is the difference between the Phillips curve constructed by A.W. Phillips and the one constructed by Samuelson and Solow?

2.   What is the relationship between a downward-sloping Phillips curve and stagflation?

3.   According to Milton Friedman, there are two (not one) Phillips curves. How does Friedman come to this conclusion?

4.   Give an example to illustrate the difference between adaptive and rational expectations.

5.   Why is the Friedman natural rate theory sometimes referred to as the fooling theory?

6.   If policy is unanticipated, does it matter to the economic outcome whether or not people hold adaptive or rational expectations? Explain your answer.

7.   If policy is correctly anticipated, does it matter to the economic outcome whether or not people hold adaptive or rational expectations? Explain your answer.

8.   What is the essence of real business cycle theory?

9.   What is the policy ineffectiveness proposition?

10. What are two assumptions in New Keynesian theory?

11. Is it possible that changes in Real GDP can originate on either the demand-side or supply-side of the economy? Explain your answer.

Problems

1.   Fill in the blank spaces in the table.

Starting point	People hold	Change in the economy	Change is	Prices and wages are	Short run change in Real GDP (rise, fall, remain unchanged)	Long run change in the price level (rise, fall, remain unchanged)
Long-run equilibrium	adaptive expectations	AD rises	unanticipated	flexible		
Long-run equilibrium	rational expectations	AD rises	correctly anticipated	flexible		
Long-run equilibrium	rational expectations	AD rises	unanticipated	flexible		

2. The economy is on the long-run Phillips curve when aggregate demand rises. If people hold adaptive expectations, draw the point the economy will move to on the short-run Phillips curve.

Inflation
Rate

Unemployment Rate

3. The economy is on the long-run Phillips curve when aggregate demand rises. If expectations are rational, and wages and prices are flexible, show where the economy will move to on either the short-run or long-run Phillips curve.

Inflation
Rate

Unemployment Rate

4. The economy is initially in long-run equilibrium when aggregate demand rises. Expectations are rational, the change in aggregate demand is correctly anticipated, but some wages and prices are inflexible. Diagrammatically represent where the economy will move to in the short run (in terms of the AD-AS diagram) and contrast this position with where the economy would move to if wages and prices were flexible.

Price
Level

Real GDP

5. Real GDP is lower in Year 2 than in Year 1. Is this because the aggregate demand curve has fallen between Year 1 and Year 2? As an aside, there is evidence that the money supply has fallen between Year 1 and Year 2.

6. The economy is in long-run equilibrium. Prices and wages are flexible. Aggregate demand increases by more than people think it will increase. Expectations are rational. Diagrammatically represent the short-run change in the economy.

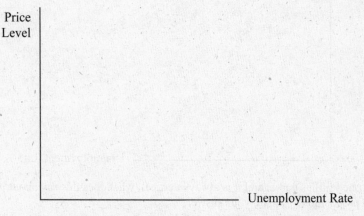

7. The economy is in long-run equilibrium. Prices and wages are flexible. Expectations are rational. Aggregate demand unexpectedly rises. Diagrammatically represent the short-run change in the economy.

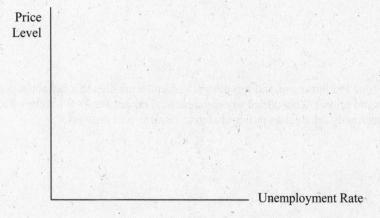

8. The economy is in long-run equilibrium. Prices are wages are flexible. Expectations are adaptive. Aggregate demand increases. Diagrammatically represent the short-run change in the economy.

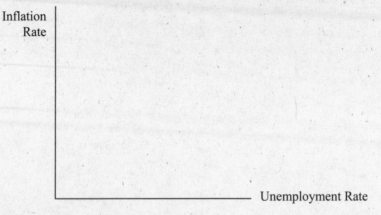

9. Diagrammatically represent the Phillips curve if there is no tradeoff between inflation and unemployment.

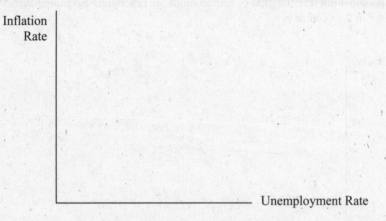

10. If there is only one Phillips curve, and it is always vertical, what does this say about the policy ineffectiveness proposition? Explain your answer.

11. If there is only one Phillips curve, and it is always vertical, what does this say about the issue of flexible wages and prices? What does it say about rational expectations? What does it say about correctly or incorrectly anticipating policy changes? Explain your answers.

What Is the Question?
Identify the question for each of the answers that follow.

1. It posited an inverse relationship between wage inflation and unemployment.

2. In the short run, the economy moves away from its natural unemployment rate, but in the long run, the economy operates at its natural unemployment rate.

3. The expected inflation rate changes faster in this theory.

4. Expectations are rational and some prices and wages are inflexible.

5. Stagflation is precluded.

6. According to this theory, there is a tradeoff between inflation and unemployment—but only in the short run.

7. Initially, both Real GDP and the price level fall. Later, the money supply may decline.

What Is Wrong?
In each of the statements that follow, something is wrong. Identify what is wrong in the space provided.

1. Stagflation over time is consistent with a short-run Phillips curve that continually shifts to the left.

2. If the economy is in long-run equilibrium, then it is not on the long-run vertical Phillips curve.

3. Rational expectations theory assumes that people are smarter today than they were yesterday, but not as smart as they will be tomorrow.

4. In real business cycle theory, LRAS shifts to the left after the money supply has fallen.

5. New Keynesian theory holds that wages are not completely flexible because of things such as rational expectations.

6. The policy ineffectiveness proposition holds under the conditions that (1) policy changes are anticipated correctly, (2) wages and prices are flexible, and (3) expectations are adaptive.

Multiple Choice

Circle the correct answer.

1. Starting from long-run equilibrium, if the public anticipates that policymakers will increase aggregate demand by less than in fact policymakers do increase aggregate demand, and if the short-run aggregate supply curve adjusts to the incorrectly anticipated increase in the aggregate demand, then
    a. Real GDP will rise and the price level will rise.
    b. Real GDP will decline and the price level will fall.
    c. Real GDP will stay constant and the price level will rise.
    d. Real GDP will fall and the price level will rise.
    e. none of the above

2. The SRAS curve will shift leftward at the same time the AD curve shifts rightward, so that there will be no change in Real GDP. This is a point that would be made by
    a. new classical economists, assuming SRAS is correctly anticipated.
    b. new classical economists, assuming AD is correctly anticipated.
    c. economists that believe in adaptive expectations theory.
    d. economists that believe that wages are inflexible in the downward direction.
    e. a and d

3. The simultaneous occurrence of high inflation and high unemployment is called
    a. reflation.
    b. stagflation.
    c. the Phillips curve dilemma.
    d. the horizontal SRAS curve paradox.
    e. none of the above

4. According to Milton Friedman, if the expected inflation rate is less than the actual inflation rate, the economy is
    a. not in long-run equilibrium.
    b. in long-run equilibrium.
    c. definitely in short-run equilibrium.
    d. a and c
    e. none of the above

5. According to the Friedman natural rate theory, there is
    a. no short-run tradeoff between inflation and unemployment.
    b. a short-run tradeoff between inflation and unemployment.
    c. no long-run tradeoff between inflation and unemployment.
    d. a and b
    e. b and c

6. According to the short-run Phillips curve,
    a. high inflation and low inflation can occur together.
    b. low unemployment and high inflation can occur together.
    c. high unemployment and high inflation can occur together.
    d. low unemployment and low inflation can occur together.
    e. a and b

7. The Phillips curve Samuelson and Solow fitted to the data was
    a. upward-sloping.
    b. vertical.
    c. downward-sloping.
    d. horizontal.
    e. none of the above

8. What is Milton Friedman's view of the Phillips curve?
    a. There is one Phillips curve and it is downward sloping.
    b. There are two Phillips curve, a vertical short-run Phillips curve and a vertical long-run Phillips curve.
    c. There is no Phillips curve.
    d. There are two Phillips curve, a short-run Phillips curve that is downward sloping and a long-run Phillips curve that is downward-sloping.
    e. none of the above

9. Which of the following would cause the economy to move from one point on the long-run Phillips curve to another point on the long-run Phillips curve?
    a. Starting from long-run equilibrium, an increase in AD, rational expectations, flexible wages and prices, and correctly anticipated changes in SRAS.
    b. Starting from long-run equilibrium, a decrease in AD, adaptive expectations, rigid wages and prices, and correctly anticipated changes in AD.
    c. Starting from long-run equilibrium, a correctly anticipated increase in AD, rigid prices and wages, and rational expectations.
    d. Starting from long-run equilibrium, a correctly anticipated increase in AD, flexible prices and wages, and rational expectations.
    e. There is not enough information to answer the question.

10. In the Friedman natural rate theory,
    a. the economy is self regulating.
    b. the economy is not self regulating.
    c. wages and prices are inflexible.
    d. rational expectations hold.
    e. a and c

11. People look to the past, present, and the future. This is most nearly consistent with
    a. adaptive expectations in the New Keynesian theory.
    b. business cycle theory.
    c. the Friedman "fooling" theory.
    d. rational expectations.
    e. the fact that Real GDP rises in the long run.

12. What will happen if wages and prices are flexible, people form their expectations rationally, and they anticipate policy incorrectly?
    a. Real GDP will change in the short run.
    b. The price level will fall in the long run.
    c. Real GDP will not change in the short run.
    d. The price level will not change in the long run.
    e. There is not enough information to answer the question.

13. New classical economists believe that when policy is unanticipated, there is a tradeoff between inflation and unemployment in
    a. the long run, but not the short run.
    b. neither the long run nor the short run.
    c. in the short run, but not the long run.
    d. both in the short run and the long run.
    e. There is not enough information to answer the question.

14. In the 1960s,
    a. there was a tradeoff between inflation and unemployment.
    b. there was no tradeoff between inflation and unemployment.
    c. stagflation existed.
    d. there was no inflation.
    e. none of the above

15. Under New Keynesian theory, a fully anticipated increase in aggregate demand will lead to _____ in Real GDP and _____ in the price level in the short run.
    a. a decrease; a decrease
    b. no change; an increase
    c. no change; no change
    d. an increase; an increase
    e. an increase; no change

True-False
Write "T" or "F" after each statement.

16. If the Phillips curve is upward-sloping, stagflation is not a possibility. _____

17. Policy is likely to be ineffective (PIP exists) if wages are inflexible in the downward direction. _____

18. Under some conditions, a rise in aggregate demand can throw the economy into a recessionary gap. _____

19. In real business cycle theory, a decrease in Real GDP is prompted by a decrease in investment. _____

20. What to some people looks like a demand-induced decrease in Real GDP and rise in unemployment could be a supply-induced decrease in Real GDP and rise in the unemployment rate. _____

Fill in the Blank
Write the correct word in the blank.

21. According to Milton Friedman, if the expected inflation rate equals the actual inflation rate, the economy is in _____ – _____ _____.

22. _____ is the simultaneous occurrence of high rates of inflation and unemployment.

23. _____ _____ economists argue that if policy is correctly anticipated, individuals form their expectations rationally, and wages and prices are flexible, then neither expansionary fiscal or monetary policy will be able to change the unemployment rate in the short run.

24. Real business cycle contractions originate on the _____ – _____ of the economy.

25. According to _____ _____ _____, individuals form their expectations rationally and wages and prices are flexible.

Chapter 16
Economic Growth

What This Chapter Is About
This chapter is about economic growth, one of the most important topics in the study of macroeconomics. This chapter discusses economic growth, per capital economic growth, and the causes and effects of economic growth.

Key Concepts in the Chapter
    a.   absolute real economic growth
    b.   per capita real economic growth

- **Absolute real economic growth** refers to an increase in Real GDP from one period to the next.
- **Per capita real economic growth** refers to an increase in per capita Real GDP from one period to the next. Per capita Real GDP is Real GDP divided by population.

Review Questions

1. What is the difference between absolute and per capita real economic growth?

2. What does it mean if economic growth occurs from an inefficient level of production?

3. What does it mean if economic growth occurs from an efficient level of production?

4. What does it mean to say "natural resources are neither a sufficient nor a necessary factor for growth"?

5. What is human capital?

6. How can capital investment lead to increases in labor productivity?

7. What do property rights refer to?

8. What two resources did neoclassical growth theory emphasize?

9. New growth theory holds that technology is endogenous. What does this mean?

10. What role do ideas play in new growth theory?

11. Paul Romer said "economic growth occurs whenever people take resources and rearrange them in ways that are more valuable." What does this mean?

12. Can economic growth affect the price level? Explain your answer.

Problems

1. Fill in the blanks in the table.

If the annual growth rate in Real GDP is	then it will take _____ years for the economy to double in size.
3 percent	
4 percent	
5 percent	

2. Diagrammatically represent economic growth from an inefficient level of production (within the PPF framework).

Capital
Goods

Consumer Goods

3. Diagrammatically represent economic growth from an efficient level of production (within the PPF framework).

Capital
Goods

Consumer Goods

4. Diagrammatically represent economic growth from an efficient level of production (within the AD-AS framework).

Price
Level

Real GDP

5. Diagrammatically represent economic growth from an inefficient level of production (within the AD-AS framework).

Price
Level

                                                                    Real GDP

6. Country X has experienced both a constant price level and absolute real economic growth (from an efficient level of production). Show this diagrammatically.

Price
Level

                                                                    Real GDP

7. Country Y has experienced both a rising price level and absolute real economic growth (from an efficient level of production). Show this diagrammatically.

Price
Level

                                                                    Real GDP

What Is the Question?
Identify the question for each of the answers that follow.

1.   Real GDP divided by population.

2.   This type of economic growth shifts the LRAS curve rightward.

3.   It makes it possible to obtain more output from the same amount of resources.

4.   It emphasized both capital and labor.

5.   According to this theory, technology is endogenous.

6.   He asks us to think about technology the way we think about prospecting for gold.

What Is Wrong?
In each of the statements that follow, something is wrong. Identify what is wrong in the space provided.

1.   Absolute real economic growth refers to an increase in per capita GDP from one period to the next.

2.   Economic growth can occur from below, on, or from beyond the production possibilities frontier.

3. Economic growth that occurs from an inefficient level of production shifts the LRAS curve to the right.

4. Countries rich in natural resources will grow faster than countries poor in natural resources.

5. According to neoclassical growth theory, technology is endogenous; according to new growth theory, technology is exogenous.

Multiple Choice
Circle the correct answer.

1. Economic growth occurring from an efficient level of production is usually portrayed as a
    a. rightward shift in the PPF.
    b. rightward shift in the LRAS curve.
    c. movement from one point below the PPF to a point on the PPF.
    d. a and b
    e. b and c

2. If an economy's Real GDP grows at 2.4 percent annually, then Real GDP will double in how many years?
    a. 30 years
    b. 15 years
    c. 10 years
    d. 8 years
    e. There is not enough information to answer the question.

3. How is per capita Real GDP computed?
    a. Real GDP multiplied by population.
    b. Real GDP adjusted for prices.
    c. Real GDP divided by population.
    d. Real GDP multiplied by GDP.
    e. none of the above

4. If the rate of economic growth slowed from 6 percent to 3 percent per year, how many additional years would it take for Real GDP to double?
    a. 12 years
    b. 24 years
    c. 8 years
    d. 5 years
    e. There is not enough information to answer the question.

5. If the economy is operating below its PPF, then any economic growth that takes place is said to occur from
    a. an efficient level of production.
    b. an inefficient level or production.
    c. a decrease in population.
    d. an increase in labor productivity.
    e. b and d

6. Which of the following will contribute to economic growth?
    a. technological advance
    b. increase in labor productivity
    c. increase in the labor force
    d. increase in capital
    e. all of the above

7. Total output is $4,000 billion worth of goods and services and total labor hours equal 200 billion. Average productivity (per hour) equals
    a. $20
    b. $80
    c. $2
    d. $4
    e. There is not enough information to answer the question.

8. Meta-ideas relate to
    a. the methods of producing ideas.
    b. persuading people that some ideas are more important than other ideas.
    c. quantifying ideas for economic use.
    d. simplifying ideas.
    e. none of the above

9. Suppose an economy produces $6,000 billion worth of output using 300 billion labor hours. If an additional person enters the economy and produces $30 worth of output, she causes _____ real economic growth.
    a. absolute, but not per capita,
    b. per capital, but not absolute,
    c. absolute and per capita
    d. neither absolute nor per capita

10. Some economists have argued that per capita real economic growth first appeared in areas where
    a. credit did not exist.
    b. property rights were established.
    c. resources were used as means instead of ends.
    d. b and c
    e. none of the above

11. An intangible factor in producing economic growth is
    a. money.
    b. capital.
    c. property rights.
    d. labor.
    e. b and c

12. The economist credited with pioneering new growth theory is
    a. Milton Friedman.
    b. John Maynard Keynes.
    c. Robert Solow.
    d. Robert Barro.
    e. Paul Romer.

13. Paul Romer would probably agree with which of the following statements?
    a. The two most important factors in economic growth are capital and labor.
    b. Economic growth is affected by the number and quality of ideas.
    c. Technology does not influence economic growth.
    d. Labor is more important than capital when it comes to economic growth.
    e. b and d

14. Economic growth can be promoted by
    a. demand-side policies, but not supply-side policies.
    b. supply-side policies, but not demand-side policies.
    c. both supply-side policies and demand-side policies.
    d. neither supply-side policies nor demand-side policies.

15. Countries rich in natural resources are
    a. guaranteed economic growth.
    b. likely to grow slower than countries poor in natural resources, *ceteris paribus*.
    c. likely to grow faster than countries poor in natural resources, *ceteris paribus*.
    d. not guaranteed economic growth.
    e. c and d

True-False
Write a "T" or "F" after each statement.

16. Absolute real economic growth refers to an increase in Real GDP from one period to the next. ___

17. Economic growth can occur from an inefficient level of production, but not from an efficient level of production. ___

18. Industrial policy is a deliberate government policy of "watering the green spots," or aiding those industries that are most likely to be successful in the world marketplace. ___

19. New growth theory holds that technology is exogenous. ___

20. According to Paul Romer, discovering and implementing new ideas is what causes economic growth.
    ___

Fill in the Blank
Write the correct word in the blank.

21. The price level will _____ if economic growth occurs from an efficient level of production and the AD curve shifts rightward more than the LRAS curve shifts rightward.

22. The price level will _____ if economic growth occurs from an inefficient level of production and the AD curve shifts rightward.

23. To calculate the time required for any variable to double, simply divide its percentage growth rate into 72. This is called the _____ _____ _____.

24. Per capita Real GDP is Real GDP divided by _____.

25. A movement from the area below the PPF to a point on the PPF represents economic growth from an _____ level of production.

Chapter 17
International Trade

What This Chapter Is About
This chapter is about international trade—why people in different countries trade with each other, the effects of tariffs and quotas, and more.

Key Concepts in the Chapter
    a. comparative advantage
    b. consumers' surplus
    c. producers' surplus

- **Comparative advantage** is the situation in which a country can produce a good at lower opportunity cost than another country.
- **Consumers' surplus** is the difference between the maximum buying price and the price paid.
- **Producers' surplus** is the difference between the price received (by the seller) and the minimum selling price.

Review Questions

1. Why do people in different countries trade with each other?

2. Why are countries better off specializing and trading (with each other) than not specializing and not trading?

3. How will a tariff affect (domestic) consumers' surplus?

4.   How will a quota affect (domestic) producers' surplus?

5.   Why might quotas be imposed even when the benefits of quotas (to the beneficiaries) are less than the costs of the quotas?

6.   Outline the details of the infant-industry argument for trade restrictions.

7.   What is the antidumping argument for trade restrictions?

8.   Suppose a tariff or quota saves some domestic jobs. Would an economist say it is worth it? Explain your answer.

9. What is the role of the WTO?

10. There is a net loss from tariffs. What does this mean?

Problems

1. Fill in the blank spaces in the second table, based on the information in the first table.

Country A can produce these combinations of X and Y	Country B can produce these combinations of X and Y
120X, 0Y	60X, 0Y
80X, 60Y	40X, 20Y
40X, 120Y	20X, 40Y
0X, 180Y	0X, 60Y

Opportunity cost of one unit of X for Country A	Opportunity cost of one unit of Y for Country A	Opportunity cost of one unit of X for Country B	Opportunity cost of one unit of Y for Country B

2. Using the diagram that follows, identify the area of consumers' surplus.

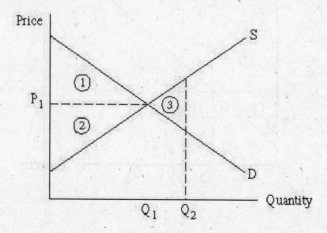

3. Using the diagram that follows, identify the area of producers' surplus.

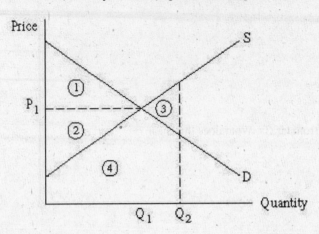

4. In the diagram (that follows), the world price is P_W. The price after a tariff has been imposed is P_T. Identify the change in consumers' surplus due to the tariff. Identify the change in producers' surplus due to the tariff.

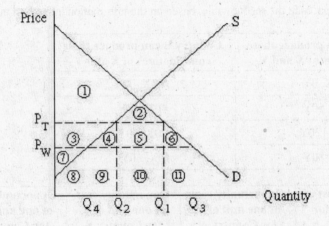

5. In the diagram (that follows), identify the gain due to the tariff. Next, identify the loss due to the tariff.

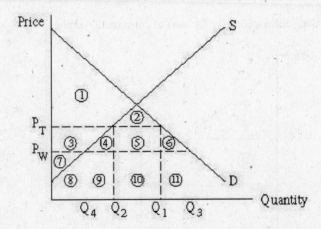

6. In the diagram (that follows), identify the net loss due to the tariff.

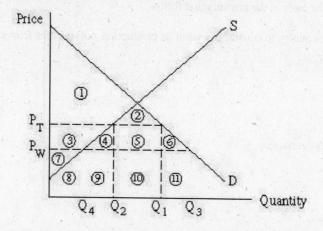

7. In the diagram (that follows), P_W is the world price and P_Q is the price after a quota has been imposed. Identify the increase in additional revenue received by importers due to the quota.

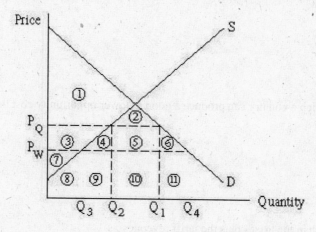

8. Using the diagram that follows, fill in the blank spaces in the table below.

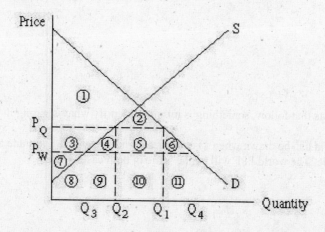

Price after quota	Loss in consumers' surplus due to the quota	Gain in producers' surplus due to the quota	Increase in revenue received by importers due to the quota	Net loss due to the quota
P_Q				

What Is the Question?
Identify the questions for each of the answers that follow.

1.   This will allow the country to consume beyond its production possibilities frontier (PPF).

2.   As a result, imports decrease.

3.   The sale of goods abroad at a price below their cost and below the price charged in the domestic market.

4.   The situation in which a country can produce a good at lower opportunity cost than another country.

5.   The gains are less than the losses plus the tariff revenues.

What Is Wrong?
In each of the statements that follow, something is missing. Identify what is wrong in the space provided.

1.   A PPF for the world can be drawn when 1) countries do not specialize and trade and 2) when they do specialize and trade. The world PPF will be the same in both cases.

2. The national-defense argument states that certain goods are necessary to the national defense and therefore should be produced only by allies.

3. A quota raises more government revenue than a tariff.

4. Consumers' surplus and producers' surplus fall as a result of a tariff being imposed on imported goods.

5. What producers gain from a quota is greater than what consumers lose from a quota.

6. If the United States sells a good for less in France than it does in Brazil, then the United States is said to be dumping goods in France.

7. A voluntary export restraint is an agreement between two countries in which importing countries voluntarily agree to limit their imports of a good from another country.

8. A quota is a tax on the amount of a good that may be imported into a country.

Multiple Choice
Circle the correct answer.

EXHIBIT A

United States		Japan	
Good X	Good Y	Good X	Good Y
120	0	30	0
80	10	20	10
40	20	10	20
0	30	0	30

1. In Exhibit A, the opportunity cost of one unit of Y for the United States is _____, whereas the opportunity cost of one unit of Y for Japan is _____.
    a. 2X; 5X
    b. 10X; 2X
    c. 4X; 1X
    d. 6X; 5X
    e. none of the above

2. In Exhibit A, the United States is the lower opportunity cost producer of _____ and Japan is the lower opportunity cost producer of _____.
    a. good X; good Y
    b. both goods; neither good
    c. neither good; both goods.
    d. good Y; good X

3. Considering the data in Exhibit A, which of the following terms of trade would both countries agree to?
    a. 5.5X = 1Y
    b. 0.5X = 1Y
    c. 5X = 1Y
    d. 2X = 1Y

4. Jack paid $40 for good X and gained $10 consumers' surplus. What is the highest price Jack would have paid for the good?
    a. $50
    b. $30
    c. $60
    d. $65
    e. There is not enough information to answer the question.

5. Producers' surplus is the difference between the price _____ receive for a good and the _____ price for which they would have _____ the good.
    a. sellers; minimum; sold
    b. buyers; maximum; bought
    c. sellers; maximum; sold
    d. buyers; minimum; bought

6. The national defense argument for trade restriction contends that
    a. the president should have the authority to erect trade barriers in case of war or national emergency.
    b. free trade makes a country dependent on other countries and this weakens the national defense.
    c. a country should produce those goods necessary fro national defense purposes even if it doesn't have a comparative advantage in them.
    d. if your enemy erects trade restrictions, so should you.
    e. b and c

7. Dumping refers to
   a. buying goods at low prices in foreign countries and selling them at high prices in the United States.
   b. expensive goods being sold for low prices.
   c. government actions to remedy "unfair" trade practices.
   d. the sale of goods abroad at a price below their cost and below the price charged in the domestic market.

8. A tariff is a
   a. restriction on the number of people that can work in an export business.
   b. legal limit on the amount of a good that may be imported.
   c. business fee incurred to ship goods abroad.
   d. tax on imports.
   e. none of the above

9. Under a policy of prohibiting exports,
   a. domestic consumers have greater consumers' surplus than under a policy of permitting exports.
   b. domestic consumers have less consumers' surplus than under a policy of permitting exports.
   c. domestic producers have greater producers' surplus than under a policy of permitting exports.
   d. a and c
   e. b and c

10. Under a tariff policy,
   a. domestic consumers have greater consumers' surplus than under a policy of free trade.
   b. domestic consumers have less consumers' surplus than under a policy of free trade.
   c. domestic producers have greater producers' surplus than under a policy of free trade.
   d. a and c
   e. b and c

11. Company A is a new company that produces a good that is already produced in many foreign countries and sold in the United States. Most likely, the argument it will voice in its attempt to be protected from foreign competition is the
   a. antidumping argument.
   b. low-foreign-wages argument.
   c. job creating argument.
   d. infant industry argument.
   e. national defense argument.

12. Tariffs and quotas are
   a. beneficial for producers in a protected industry, but not beneficial for the workers in the industry.
   b. beneficial for producers in a protected industry, but not beneficial for consumers.
   c. beneficial for workers in a protected industry, but not beneficial for consumers.
   d. not beneficial for the workers in a protected industry or for consumers.
   e. b and c

13. A tariff is imposed on good X. The tariff will _____ the price of good X in the domestic market, _____ the number of units of good X imported into the domestic market, and _____ consumers' surplus.
   a. lower; raise; raise
   b. raise; lower; lower
   c. raise; lower; raise
   d. lower; raise; lower
   e. none of the above

14. Tariffs and quotas are often imposed when government is responsive to _____ interests, and the benefits of tariffs and quotas are often _____.
    a.   consumer; dispersed
    b.   consumer; concentrated
    c.   producer; dispersed
    d.   producer; concentrated

15. Which of the following is not an example of a trade restriction?
    a.   tariff
    b.   quota
    c.   dumping
    d.   a and b
    e.   a, b, and c

True-False
Write "T" or "F" at the end of each statement.

16. Consumers' surplus is greater at higher prices than lower prices. _____

17. There is a net loss from tariffs. _____

18. Specialization and trade allow a country's inhabitants to consume at a level beyond its production possibilities frontier. _____

19. If the price received is $40 and producers' surplus is $10, then the minimum selling price is $30. _____

20. A quota is a legal limit on the amount of a good that may be imported. _____

Fill in the Blank
Write the correct word in the blank.

21. The _____ argument states that domestic producers should not have to compete (on an unequal basis) with foreign producers that sell products below cost and below the prices they charge in their domestic markets.

22. As a result of a quota, the number of imported goods will _____.

23. As a result of a tariff, consumers' surplus _____.

24. The gains from a quota are _____ than the losses from a quota.

25. The gains from free trade are _____ than the losses from protected (non-free) trade.

Chapter 18
International Finance

What This Chapter Is About
The main subject of this chapter is exchange rates. What are exchange rates? How are exchange rates determined? What are the effects of changes in exchange rates? These questions and more are answered in this chapter.

Key Concepts in the Chapter
- a. balance of payments
- b. current account balance
- c. capital account balance
- d. merchandise trade balance
- e. exchange rate
- f. appreciation
- g. depreciation
- h. optimal currency area

- The **balance of payments** is a periodic statement of the money value of all transactions between residents of one country and residents of all other countries.
- The **current account balance** is the summary statistic for exports of goods and services, imports of goods and services, and net unilateral transfers abroad.
- The **capital account balance** is the summary statistic for the outflow of U.S. capital and the inflow of foreign capital. It is equal to the difference between the outflow of U.S. capital and the inflow of foreign capital.
- The **merchandise trade balance** is the difference between the value of merchandise exports and the value of merchandise imports.
- The **exchange rate** is the price of one currency in terms of another currency.
- **Appreciation** refers to an increase in the value of one currency relative to other currencies.
- **Depreciation** refers to a decrease in the value of one currency relative to other currencies.
- An **optimal currency area** is a geographic area in which exchange rates can be fixed or a common currency used without sacrificing domestic economic goals—such as low unemployment.

Review Questions

1. Give an example of a transaction that would be considered a debit item in the balance of payments.

2. Give an example of a transaction that would be considered a credit item in the balance of payments.

3. What is the difference between the current account balance and the merchandise trade balance?

4. What items compose the capital account?

5. What is the difference between a flexible and a fixed exchange rate system?

6. The demand for pounds is related to the supply of dollars. How so?

7. The supply of pounds is related to the demand for dollars. How so?

8. It took 106 yen to buy 1 dollar on Tuesday and 110 yen to buy 1 dollar on Wednesday. Has the dollar appreciated or depreciated from Tuesday to Wednesday? Explain your answer.

9. What factors can lead to a change in exchange rates?

10. Give an example of a currency that is overvalued.

11. What is the difference between a currency that is devalued and one that has depreciated?

Problems

Answer questions 1 through 5 based on the table that follows.

Item	Dollar amount
Merchandise exports	+ 400
Income from U.S. assets abroad	+ 36
Services (exports)	+ 80
Outflow of U.S. capital	− 33
Statistical discrepancy	− 20
Inflow of foreign capital	+ 50
Increase in U.S. official reserve assets	− 5
Decrease in foreign official assets in the U.S.	+ 4
Merchandise imports	− 410
Services (imports)	− 34
Net unilateral transfers abroad	− 18
Income from foreign assets in U.S.	− 50

1. What does the merchandise trade balance equal?

2. What does the current account balance equal?

3. What does the capital account balance equal?

4. What does the official reserve balance equal?

5. What does the balance of payments equal?

6. Suppose there are only two currencies in the world, pesos and dollars. Fill in the blank spaces in the table.

If the	Then the
demand for dollars rises in the foreign exchange market	
	supply of dollars falls on the foreign exchange market
	supply of pesos rises on the foreign exchange market

7. Fill in the blank spaces where a question mark appears in the table.

If	Then
$1 = 106 yen	1 yen = ?
$1 = 74 Kenyan shillings	1 shilling = ?
$1 = 1,500 Lebanese pounds	1 pound = ?

8. Fill in the blank spaces in the table.

The exchange rate is	And the item costs	What does the item cost in dollars?
$1 = 106 yen	18,000 yen	
$1 = £0.50	£ 34.00	
$1 = 9.44 pesos	89 pesos	

9. Fill in the blank spaces in the table.

The exchange rate changes from	Has the dollar appreciated or depreciated?
$2 = £1 to $2.50 = £1	
109 yen = $1 to 189 yen = $1	
10 pesos = $1 to 8 pesos = $1	

10. Fill in the blank spaces in the table.

If ...	The dollar will (appreciate, depreciate)
the real interest rate in the U.S. rises relative to real interest rates in other countries	
income in foreign countries (that trade with the U.S.) rises relative to income in the United States	
the inflation rate in the U.S. rises and the inflation rate in all other countries falls	

11. Fill in the blank spaces in the table.

If the equilibrium exchange rate is $1 = £ 0.50 and the official exchange rate is	Then the dollar is (overvalued, undervalued)
$1 = £ 0.60	
$1 = £ 0.30	

What Is the Question?
Identify the question for each of the answers that follow.

1. Any transaction that supplies the country's currency in the foreign exchange market.

2. Any transaction that creates a demand for the country's currency in the foreign exchange market.

3. The summary statistic for the exports of goods and services, imports of goods and services, and net unilateral transfers abroad.

4. The difference between the value of merchandise exports and the value of merchandise imports.

5. One-way money payments.

6. The price of one currency in terms of another currency.

7. It predicts that the exchange rates between any two currencies will adjust to reflect changes in the relative price levels of the two countries.

8.   Raising the official price of a currency.

What Is Wrong?
In each of the statements that follow, something is wrong. Identify what is wrong in the space provided.

1.   The balance of payments is the summary statistic for the current account balance, capital account balance, net unilateral transfers abroad, and statistical discrepancy.

2.   The demand for dollars on the foreign exchange market is linked to the supply of dollars on the foreign exchange market. In short, if the demand for dollars rises, the supply of dollars rises, too.

3.   There are two countries, A and B. The income of Country B rises and the income of Country A remains constant. As a result, the currency of Country B appreciates.

4.   There are two countries, C and D. The price level in Country C rises 10 percent and the inflation rate in Country D is zero percent. As a result, the demand for Country C's goods rises, and the supply of its currency falls.

5.   A change in real interest rates across countries cannot change the exchange rate.

6.   If the equilibrium exchange rate is £1 = $1.50, and the official exchange rate is £1 = $1.60, then the dollar is overvalued and the pound is undervalued.

7.   An international monetary fund right is a special international money created by the IMF.

Multiple Choice
Circle the correct answer.

1. An international transaction that supplies the nation's currency also creates a
    a. supply of foreign currency, and is recorded as a credit in the balance of payments.
    b. demand for foreign currency, and is recorded as a credit in the balance of payments.
    c. demand for foreign currency, and is recorded as a debit in the balance of payments.
    d. supply of the nation's currency, and is recorded as a debit in the balance of payments.

2. If the French buy American computers, they
    a. demand U.S. dollars and supply French francs.
    b. demand U.S. dollars and demand French francs.
    c. supply U.S. dollars and demand French francs.
    d. supply both U.S. dollars and French francs.

Exhibit A

Components of the Balance of Payments	($ billions)
Exports of goods and services	+ 330
Merchandise exports (including military sales)	+ 150
Export services	+ 40
Income from U.S. assets abroad	+ 140
Imports of goods and services	− 390
Merchandise imports (including military sales)	− 220
Import services	− 80
Income from foreign assets abroad	− 90
Net unilateral transfers abroad	− 21
Outflow of U.S. capital	− 46
Inflow of foreign capital	+ 60
Increase in U.S. official reserve assets	− 21
Increase in foreign official assets in U.S.	+ 23
Statistical discrepancy	+ 65

3. In Exhibit A, the merchandise trade balance equals _____ billion dollars.
    a. − 80
    b. + 100
    c. − 70
    d. + 60
    e. none of the above

4. In Exhibit A, the current account balance equals _____ billion dollars.
    a. − 111
    b. − 81
    c. − 60
    d. + 63
    e. none of the above

5. In Exhibit A, the capital account balance equals _____ billion dollars.
    a. + 15
    b. − 10
    c. + 14
    d. − 14
    e. none of the above

6. In Exhibit A, the official reserve balance equals _____ billion dollars.
   a. + 2
   b. − 1
   c. + 10
   d. + 17
   e. none of the above

7. The three major components of the current account are
   a. exports of goods and services, imports of goods and services, and statistical discrepancy.
   b. outflow of U.S. foreign capital, inflow of foreign capital, and statistical discrepancy.
   c. merchandise exports, merchandise imports, and net unilateral transfers abroad.
   d. exports of goods and services, imports of goods and services, and inflow of foreign capital.
   e. none of the above

8. The lower the dollar price per yen, the _____ Japanese goods are for Americans and the _____
   Japanese goods Americans will buy; thus _____ yen will be demanded.
   a. more expensive; more; fewer
   b. more expensive; fewer; fewer
   c. less expensive; more; more
   d. less expensive; more; fewer
   e. none of the above

9. An American computer is priced at $5,500. If the exchange rate between the U.S. dollar and the British
   pound is $1.70 = £1, approximately how many pounds will a British buyer pay for the computer?
   a. £3,235
   b. £3,052
   c. £2,543
   d. £6,599

10. If the dollar price per pound moves from $1.90 = £1 to $1.40 = £1, the pound is said to have _____
    and the dollar to have _____.
    a. depreciated; appreciated
    b. appreciated; appreciated
    c. appreciated; depreciated
    d. depreciated; depreciated

11. The U.S. dollar has appreciated relative to the French franc if it takes
    a. fewer francs to buy a dollar.
    b. fewer dollars to buy a franc.
    c. more dollars to buy a franc.
    d. a and c
    e. none of the above

12. Suppose the current exchange rate between the dollar and British pound is $1.70 = £1. Furthermore,
    suppose the price level in the United States rises 25 percent at a time when the British price level is
    stable. According to the purchasing power parity theory, what will be the new equilibrium exchange
    rate?
    a. $2.72 = £1
    b. $1.55 = £1
    c. $1.86 = £1
    d. $2.13 = £1

13. The purchasing power parity theory predicts less nearly accurately in the _____ run, and when there is a _____ difference in inflation rates across countries.
    a. long; small
    b. short; large
    c. long; large
    d. short; small

14. Under a fixed exchange rate system, if the Mexican peso is overvalued then there exists
    a. a shortage of pesos.
    b. a surplus of pesos.
    c. the equilibrium level of pesos.
    d. There is not enough information to answer the question (we need to know the actual exchange rate).

15. One of the things a nation must do if it is on an international gold standard is
    a. link its money supply to its gold holdings.
    b. increase taxes.
    c. declare itself to be on a flexible exchange rate system.
    d. revalue its currency.
    e. none of the above

True-False
Write "T" or "F" after each statement.

16. If more euros are needed to buy a dollar, then the dollar has appreciated. ____

17. If fewer euros are needed to buy a peso, the euro has depreciated. ____

18. Any transaction that supplies the nation's currency is recorded as a debit in the balance of payments. ____

19. The current account balance is the summary statistic for exports of goods and services, imports of goods and services, and the statistical discrepancy. ____

20. Any transaction that supplies a foreign currency is recorded as a credit in the balance of payments. ____

Fill in the Blank
Write the correct word in the blank.

21. The _____ _____ _____ is the difference between the value of merchandise exports and the value of merchandise imports.

22. The _____ _____ _____ _____ predicts that changes in the relative price levels of two countries will affect the exchange rate in such a way that one unit of nation's currency will continue to buy the same amount of foreign goods as it did before the change in the relative price levels.

23. When nations adopt the gold standard, they automatically _____ their exchange rates.

24. A _____ occurs when the official price of currency (under the fixed exchange rate system) is lowered.

25. Central banks play a much larger role under a _____ exchange rate system than under a _____ exchange rate system.

Chapter 19
Globalization and International Impacts on the Economy

What This Chapter Is About
This chapter is about the costs and the benefits of globalization and the international impacts on the economy.

Key Concepts in the Chapter
- a. globalization
- b. offshoring
- c. J-curve
- d. closed economy
- e. open economy

- **Globalization** is a phenomenon by which economic agents in any given part of the world are more affected by events elsewhere in the world than before; it refers to the growing integration of the national economies of the world to the degree that we may be witnessing the emergence and operation of a single worldwide economy.
- **Offshoring** is the term used to describe work done for a company by persons other than the company's original employees in a country other than the one in which the company is located.
- A **J-curve** shows a short-run worsening in net exports after a currency depreciation, followed later by an improvement.
- A **closed economy** is an economy that does not trade goods and services with other countries.
- An **open economy** is an economy that does trade goods and services with other countries.

Review Questions

1. Globalization is a process by which the world "becomes smaller." What does this mean?

2. Give an example of something happening in one country that affects the people in another country.

3. Identify and explain the two ways (identified in the text) with which to "see" globalization.

4.   Is globalization unique to the end of the 20th century and beginning of the 21st century?

5.   What is the "end-of-the-Cold-War" explanation for current globalization?

6.   How can technological advancements promote globalization?

7.   Give an example of an economic policy that acts to retard globalization.

8.   Identify a few of the potential benefits of globalization.

9. When it comes to globalization, it is often much more difficult to see the benefits than the costs. Why?

10. How might a change in foreign real national income affect U.S. GDP?

11. Explain how dollar appreciation will affect the prices of foreign goods purchased by Americans.

12. Explain how dollar depreciation will affect both U.S. imports and exports.

13. How does the discussion of the J-curve illustrate that economists think in terms of both the short run and the long run?

14. How does a change in foreign input prices affect the U.S. SRAS curve?

15. Identify two reasons why foreign input prices may change for Americans.

16. A change in the international value of the dollar can change both the AD and SRAS curves in the United States, so what is the overall effect on the U.S. price level?

17. How will higher real interest rates in the U.S. affect the international value of the dollar?

18. Identify a few of the international effects of higher U.S. budget deficits.

19. Identify the international effects of contractionary U.S. monetary policy.

What Is the Question?
Identify the question for each of the answers that follow.

1. During a rather intense period of globalization during the 1990s and early 2000s, the unemployment rate in the U.S. was low.

2. Forty percent in 1946 and about 1.4 percent today.

3. In 1995 it was 60 times higher than it was in 1977.

4. The end of the Cold War.

5. The end of the Cold War, technological changes that lower the costs of transporting goods and communicating with people, and government policy changes that express an openness toward freer markets and long-distance trade.

6. Because the benefits are spread over many people and the costs are concentrated on relatively few.

7. Exports minus imports.

8. The J-curve.

9. A change in supply and demand conditions and a change in exchange rates.

10. This shifts the AD curve rightward and the SRAS curve leftward.

11. There are no international feedback effects in this type of economy.

12. The type of fiscal policy that lowers Real GDP more in a closed economy than in an open economy.

13. The type of monetary policy that lowers Real GDP more in an open economy than in a closed economy.

14. The type of monetary policy that raises Real GDP more in an open economy than in a closed economy.

15. Increases capital inflows into the country.

What Is Wrong?
In each of the statements that follow, there is something wrong. Identify what is wrong in the space provided.

1. Globalization is closely aligned with a movement toward more free enterprise, restrained markets, and more freedom of government for people and goods.

2. Tariff rates are higher in the United States today than they were in 1946.

3. The cost of a three-minute telephone call from New York to London was $250; in 2000, it was $10.

4. Between 1980 and 2000, income per person increased 20 percent in India.

5. Between 1990 and 2005, the CPI rose more slowly than the import price index.

6. Globalization causes greater income inequality.

7. The benefits of globalization tend to be difficult to see, partly because they are so concentrated.

8. Expansionary fiscal policy shifts the AD curve rightward (and under certain conditions) raises Real GDP. If the expansionary fiscal policy causes a deficit, then the government will have to borrow to finance the deficit, and interest rates will be pushed downward.

9. When the money supply is raised, the AD curve shifts rightward, pushing up Real GDP. Also, as a result of the increased money supply, interest rates may decline in the short run. This leads to U.S. capital inflow and an appreciated dollar.

10. To finance the growing budget deficit, the U.S. Treasury borrows more funds in the credit (or loanable funds) market than it would have borrowed if the latest spending had been passed.

11. The phenomenon in which import spending initially rises after an appreciation and then later falls is summarized in the J-curve.

12. A change in the exchange rate will change the AD curve in an open economy.

Multiple Choice
Circle the correct answer.

1. A characteristic of globalization is
    a. a greater world population.
    b. a greater number of economic links with people outside the country.
    c. a physically smaller world.
    d. less offshoring.
    e. a and b

2. Globalization was occurring between 1990 and 2006. If globalization takes jobs away from Americans (without replacing them, in whole or in part), then we would expect to see during this period
    a. a declining unemployment rate.
    b. a rising unemployment rate.
    c. declining U.S. ownership of foreign stocks.
    d. less foreign direct investment.
    e. none of the above

3. As evidence of increased globalization,
    a. in 2000 the average tariff was 18.7 percent and one year later it was lower.
    b. daily foreign trading has increased.
    c. fewer countries are members of the WTO.
    d. a and b
    e. b and c

4. Which of the following statements is false?
    a. During the period from the mid-1800s to the late-1920s, globalization was occurring.
    b. According to Thomas Friedman, globalization is not an economic fad.
    c. Globalization is closely aligned with a movement toward more free enterprise, freer markets, and more freedom of movement for people and goods.
    d. The average tariff rate in the United States is higher today than it was in 1946.
    e. none of the above

5. Some of the signs of globalization include:
    a. tariff rates rising.
    b. greater foreign exchange trading.
    c. less foreign direct investment.
    d. more residents in one country working for companies located in other countries.
    e. b and d

6. The Internet is most likely something that
    a. does not affect globalization.
    b. promotes globalization.
    c. leads to a change in government policy toward more protectionism.
    d. b and c
    e. none of the above

7. Some of the benefits of globalization often cited include:
    a. friendlier relations between countries.
    b. a homogeneous world culture.
    c. higher income per person.
    d. less stressful life.
    e. none of the above

8. Some of the costs of globalization often cited include:
    a. increased income inequality.

    b.   offshoring (losing jobs).
    c.   more stressful life.
    d.   a and b
    e.   a, b, and c

9. A debate wages on as to whether there will be more or less globalization in the future. One of the factors that could result in less globalization is
    a.   a change in government policy toward, say, greater protectionism.
    b.   less global terrorism.
    c.   technological advances.
    d.   b and c
    e.   none of the above

10. Which of the following statements is false?
    a.   Robert Wright argues that it is not a coincidence that religious tolerance is high in the United States, a country that is open to trade and globalization.
    b.   One of the benefits of globalization is increased trade.
    c.   Between 1977 and 2004, the inflation-adjusted prices for an array of goods traded between countries increased while the inflation-adjusted prices for an array of goods not traded between countries actually decreased.
    d.   b and c
    e.   none of the above

11. Real national income rises in Country X. As a result, in Country Y the following is likely to happen:
    a.   export spending rises.
    b.   import spending falls.
    c.   export spending falls.
    d.   import spending rises.
    e.   a and b

12. If a country's currency appreciates,
    a.   it takes more of the country's currency to buy a unit of another country's currency.
    b.   it takes less of the country's currency to buy a unit of another country's currency.
    c.   another country's currency must depreciate.
    d.   a and c
    e.   b and c

13. A depreciation in the dollar and an appreciation in the yen will likely
    a.   lower U.S. exports and raise U.S. imports.
    b.   raise U.S. exports and lower U.S. imports.
    c.   shift the U.S. AD curve to the left.
    d.   increase the U.S. budget deficit.
    e.   none of the above

14. If the dollar depreciates, then foreign inputs will
    a.   increase in supply.
    b.   become cheaper for Americans.
    c.   decrease in demand.
    d.   become more expensive for Americans.
    e.   a and b

15. A larger budget deficit in the U.S. could lead to
    a.   a depreciated dollar.
    b.   an appreciated dollar.
    c.   an increase in the demand for dollars.
    d.   an increase in the supply of dollars.
    e.   b and c

16. Expansionary fiscal policy raises Real GDP
    a.   more in an open economy than in a closed economy.
    b.   more in a closed economy than in an open economy.
    c.   the same amount in both a closed economy and open economy.
    d.   less in a closed economy than in an open economy.
    e.   a and d

17. Higher real interest rates in the United States will
    a.   attract foreign capital and lead to an appreciation in the dollar.
    b.   attract foreign capital and lead to a depreciation in the dollar.
    c.   lead to foreign produced goods becoming cheaper for Americans.
    d.   a and c
    e.   b and c

18. An increase in foreign input prices will
    a.   shift the U.S. SRAS curve to the right.
    b.   shift the U.S. AD curve to the left.
    c.   shift the U.S. SRAS curve to the left.
    d.   shift the U.S AD curve to the right.
    e.   b and c

19. If the dollar depreciates, the U.S.
    a.   AD curve will shift to the right and the SRAS curve will shift to the left.
    b.   AD curve will shift to the left and the SRAS curve will shift to the right.
    c.   AD curve will shift to the right and the SRAS curve will shift to the right.
    d.   AD curve will shift to the left and the SRAS curve will shift to the left.

20. If the dollar appreciates, the U.S.
    a.   AD curve will shift to the right and the SRAS curve will shift to the left.
    b.   AD curve will shift to the left and the SRAS curve will shift to the right.
    c.   AD curve will shift to the right and the SRAS curve will shift to the right.
    d.   AD curve will shift to the left and the SRAS curve will shift to the left.

True-False
Write "T" or "F" at the end of each statement.

21. A U.K. study showed that almost three times as many firms that faced global competition reported product or process innovations than those firms that did not face global competition. _____

22. Increased income inequality is sometimes cited as one of the costs of globalization. _____

23. Globalization is often associated with less free enterprise. _____

24. Foreign direct investment relates to a company in one country investing in a company in another country. _____

25. If the dollar appreciates and the yen depreciates, then Japanese goods become more expensive for Americans and U.S. goods become less expensive for the Japanese. ____

26. If the U.S. budget deficit rises, then it can eventually lead to an appreciation in the dollar. ____

27. What happens in the U.S. credit market can affect the dollar-euro exchange rate. ____

28. Expansionary monetary policy raises Real GDP less in open economy than in a closed economy. ____

29. Contractionary fiscal policy lowers Real GDP more in a closed economy than in an open economy. ____

Fill in the Blank
Write the correct word in the blank.

30. The _____ _____ _____ is an international organization whose mission it is to promote international free trade.

31. _____ _____ by governments can affect globalization.

32. One of the benefits of globalization is _____ _____ for goods.

33. _____ is the practice of hiring people in other countries.

34. According to _____ _____ "Man is an animal that makes bargains: no other animal does this — no dog exchanges bones with another."

35. If the dollar _____, the U.S. AD curve shifts to the left and the SRAS curve shifts to the right.

36. _____ fiscal policy lowers Real GDP more in a closed economy than in an open economy.

37. If real interest rates rise in the United States, then foreign capital will flow _____ the United States.

38. _____ _____ _____ lowers Real GDP more in an open economy than in a closed economy.

39. A change in foreign inputs prices (paid for by U.S. producers) can be the result of change in the input market in the foreign country or a change in the _____ _____.

Chapter 20
Stocks, Bonds, Futures, and Options

What This Chapter Is About
In this chapter we discuss stocks, bonds, futures, and options.

Key Concepts in the Chapter
    a.   financial market
    b.   stocks
    c.   bonds
    d.   futures contract
    e.   options

- A **financial market** channels money from some people (who want to borrow) to other people (who want to lend).
- A **stock** is a claim on the assets of a corporation that gives the purchaser a share of the corporation.
- A **bond** is a debt obligation to repay a certain sum of money (the principal) at maturity and also to pay periodic fixed sums until that date.
- A **futures contract** is an agreement to buy or sell a specific amount of something (commodity, currency, financial instrument) at a particular price on a stipulated future date.
- An **option** is a contract that gives the owner the right, but not the obligation, to buy or sell shares of a stock at a specified price on or before a specified date.

Review Questions

1. A person who owns stock is an owner of a company while a person who owns a bond (issued by the company) is not. Explain.

2. What is the history of the Down Jones Industrial Average (DJIA)?

3. A company wants to raise money so that it can invest in a new product. Identify three ways it can obtain the money.

4. What is an initial public offering?

5. Why do people buy stock?

6. What is a stock index fund?

7. Are bonds all sold at their face value?

8. What is the difference between the primary and secondary bond markets?

9. Why can't the issuer of a bond set the bond's coupon rate at any percentage that he or she wants?

10. What is an inflation-indexed Treasury bond?

11. Who is likely to buy a futures contract?

12. Explain how a currency futures contract works.

13. Explain how a call option works.

14. What does a PE ratio of 13 mean?

Problems

1. If the dividend per share of stock is $4 and the closing price per share is $20, then what is the yield?

2. If the closing price per share of stock is $40 and the net earnings per share are $1.50, then what is the PE ratio equal to?

3. If the face value of a bond is $10,000 and the coupon rate is 5.4 percent, what are the annual coupon payments equal to?

4. If the price paid for a bond is less than the bond's face value, and the coupon rate of the bond is 5 percent, does it follow that the yield on the bond is higher than, lower than, or equal to the coupon rate?

5. Suppose you purchase an inflation-indexed, 10-year, $1,000 bond that pays a coupon rate of 5.2 percent. What is the annual coupon payment? If the inflation rate is 3.4 percent one year, what is the "new" value of the bond equal to?

6. Smith and Jones enter into a futures contract. Smith promises to buy $20 million of euros in six months for 77 cents per euro. Jones promises to sell $20 million of euros in six months for 77 cents per euro. Six months pass and a euro sells for 83 cents. How much money does Jones lose?

7. Yvonne puts a call option for $40. The strike price is $150. The price of the stock rises above $150. Will Yvonne exercise the call option? Explain your answer.

What Is the Question?
Identify the question for each of the answers that follow.

1. A claim on the assets of a corporation that gives the purchaser a share in the corporation.

2. May 26, 1896.

3. Thirty stocks.

4. The editors of the *Wall Street Journal*.

5. Payments made to stockholders based on a company's profits.

6. Dividend per share divided by the closing price per share of the stock.

7. The closing price per share of a stock divided by the net earnings per share.

8. The yield and price paid are inversely related.

9. The annual coupon payment divided by the price paid for the bond.

10. First issued in 1997.

11. A contract in which the seller agrees to provide a particular good to the buyer on a specified future date at an agreed-upon price.

12. A contract that gives the owner the right, but not the obligation, to buy or sell shares of a stock at a specified price on or before a specified date.

13. It will sell for a fraction of the price of the stock.

14. A stock that plunges fast and furiously, much like an airplane that hits an air pocket.

What Is Wrong?
In each of the statements that follow, there is something wrong. Identify what is wrong in the space provided.

1. An example of a broad-based stock index is the Wilshire, which consists of the stocks of about 5,000 firms.

2. The yield of a stock is equal to the dividend per share divided by the stock's PE ratio.

3. As the price for a bond falls, the yield on the bond falls too.

4. When it comes to bonds, the number after the colon (as in 105:12) stands for 16ths of $10.

5. Call options give the owner the right, but not the obligation, to sell shares of a stock at a strike price during some period of time.

Multiple Choice
Circle the correct answer.

1. A stock currently sells for $400 a share. You don't have enough money to buy many shares of the stock but you would like to benefit from (what you expect) will be an uptick in its price. To do this, you can
    a. sell a put option.
    b. buy a call option.
    c. sell a call option.
    d. enter into a futures contract.
    e. none of the above

2. A futures contract is
    a. a contract in which the seller agrees to provide a particular good to the buyer on a specified future date at an agreed-upon price.
    b. a contract in which seller agrees to buy a particular good from a buy on a specified future date at a price to be agreed-upon in the future.
    c. a contract that deals with selling a bond at a price that existed at an earlier time.
    d. the same thing as a put option.
    e. none of the above

3. The person most likely to buy a put option is a person who thinks the price of a stock is
    a. going to fall.
    b. going to rise.
    c. not going to change.
    d. a or c
    e. none of the above

4. The person most likely to sell a put option is a person who thinks the price of a stock is
    a. going to fall.
    b. going to rise.
    c. not going to change.
    d. a or c
    e. none of the above

5. The person most likely to sell a call option is the person
    a. most likely to think the option would be exercised.
    b. most likely to think the option would not be exercised.
    c. who preferred bonds to stocks.
    d. who preferred stocks to bonds.
    e. none of the above

6. It is usually the case that
    a. higher risks come with lower returns.
    b. lower returns come with constant risks.
    c. higher risks come with higher returns.
    d. returns are independent of risks.
    e. lower risks come with higher risks.

7. A bond's yield is based on the
    a. bid price.
    b. ask price.
    c. highest price.
    d. lowest price.
    e. none of the above

8. The PE ratio is equal to
    a. net earnings per share multiplied by closing price per share.
    b. closing price per share multiplied by 100.
    c. closing price per share divided by net earnings per share.
    d. closing price per share divided by 30 (the number of stocks that compose the DJIA).
    e. none of the above

9. Why you buy Spyders, you are buying the stock of
    a. 1,000 companies.
    b. 50 companies.
    c. 30 companies.
    d. 250 companies.
    e. none of the above

10. As a result of buying stock, a person is a(an)
    a. lender.
    b. borrower.
    c. consumer.
    d. owner.
    e. none of the above

True-False

Write a "T" or "F" after each statement.

11. Interest payments are payments to persons who own stock. ____

12. The DJIA is composed of 35 stocks. ____

13. If the dividend is 2.03, this means that the last annual divided per share of stock was $2.03. ____

14. Buyers of call options can buy shares of a stock at a strike price. ____

15. A person who owns a put option has the right to sell shares of a stock at a strike price. ____

Fill in the Blank

Write the correct word in the blank.

16. A _____ _____ is a slang term used to refer to a perfect stock or investment.

17. The people who think the price of a stock is going to rise are likely to sell _____

    _____.

18. A _____ is an IOU or promise to pay.

19. The _____ _____ is equal to the closing price per share of a stock divided by the net earnings per share.

20. The price of a bond and its yield move in _____ directions.

Chapter 21
Agriculture: Problems, Policies, and Unintended Effects

WEB CHAPTER

What This Chapter Is About
Various agricultural markets — the corn market, wheat market, and so on — are often put forth as examples of perfectly competitive markets. Do sellers, in perfectly competitive markets, face any unusual problems? Does government get involved in affecting outcomes in perfectly competitive markets? This chapter answers these questions and more.

Key Concepts in the Chapter
    a. price elasticity of demand
    b. income elasticity of demand
    c. price support

- **Price elasticity of demand** measures the responsiveness of a change in quantity demanded to a change in price.
- **Income elasticity of demand** measures the responsiveness of a change in quantity demanded to changes in income.
- A **price support** is a government-mandated minimum price for agricultural products; it is an example of a price floor.

Review Questions

1. If an increase in the supply of a food item lowers farmers' income, what does this say about the (price) elasticity of demand for the food item? Explain your answer.

2. What do price inelasticity of demand for a food item and major changes in the weather have to do with the fact that farmers may experience large changes in their income from year to year?

3. Why might a farmer want to enter into a futures contract?

4. An individual farmer may prefer (1) good weather for himself and bad weather for all other farmers over (2) good weather for all farmers, including himself. Why?

5. What are the effects of an agricultural price support?

6. Diagrammatically represent and explain how target prices work.

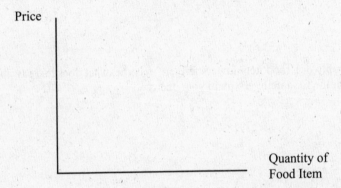

7. In 2002, the federal government replaced production flexibility contract payments with fixed direct payments, which essentially work the same way as production flexibility contract payments. How do production flexibility contract payments work.

8. Explain how a nonrecourse commodity loan works?

Problems

1. Fill in the blank spaces in the table.

If demand for the food item is	And supply of the food item	Then farmers' income (rises, falls, remains unchanged)
elastic	rises	
inelastic	rises	
inelastic	falls	

2. Fill in the blank spaces in the table.

Target price	Market price	Quantity supplied at target price	Deficiency payment
$4	$1	4,000 units	
$5	$5	3,000 units	
$6	$3	10,000 units	

3. Diagrammatically represent how a supply-restricting policy might work.

What Is the Question?
Identify the question for each of the answers that follow.

1. An obligation to make or take delivery of a specified quantity of a good at a particular time in the future at a price agreed on when the contract is signed.

2. A government-mandated minimum price for agricultural products.

3. It restricts output by limiting the number of farm acres that can be used to produce a particular crop.

4. They are similar to production flexibility contract payments and direct payments except that they are based on the difference between an effective price (established for the crop) and a target price.

5. It is a particular type of price support; in fact, it is the major way the government supports crop prices.

What Is Wrong?
In each of the statements that follow, there is something wrong. Identify what is wrong in the space provided.

1. When agricultural productivity increases, the supply of food items shifts right, price falls, and total revenue (received by farmers) rises if demand is inelastic.

2. The demand for many farm products is income inelastic, which means that quantity demanded changes by a large percentage than income changes.

3. In 2004, about 10 percent of U.S. farmers received subsidy payments.

4. Today, one farmer in the United States produces enough food to feed 100 people.

5. Income elasticity of demand measures the responsiveness of a change in quantity demanded to changes in price.

Multiple Choice
Circle the correct answer.

1. At the beginning of the century, a farmer produced enough food to feed
    a. 8 people.
    b. 17 people.
    c. 35 people.
    d. 82 people.

2. The supply curve of farm products has shifted rightward during much of the 20th century principally because of
    a. higher prices for foods.
    b. consistently good weather.
    c. increased productivity in the agricultural sector.
    d. more people going into farming.

3. Increased productivity in the agricultural sector is not always a benefit to farmers because with increased productivity comes
    a. higher prices and if demand is inelastic, then higher prices mean lower revenues.
    b. higher prices and if demand is elastic, then higher prices mean lower revenues.
    c. lower prices and if demand is elastic, then lower prices mean lower revenues.
    d. lower prices and if demand is inelastic, then lower prices mean constant revenues.
    e. lower prices and if demand is inelastic, then lower prices mean lower revenues.

4. In the United States, studies show that as real income has been rising, the per capita demand for food has been increasing by
    a. as much, which means the demand for food is unit elastic.
    b. much more, which means the demand for food is income elastic.
    c. much more, which means the demand for food is income inelastic.
    d. much less, which means the demand for food is income inelastic.
    e. none of the above

5. Why is good weather sometimes bad news for farmers?
    a. Because good weather lowers the demand for, and price of, agricultural products.
    b. Because good weather shifts the supply curve of agricultural products leftward, driving up price, and lowering total revenue (assuming demand is elastic).
    c. Because good weather shifts the supply curve of agricultural products rightward, driving down price and total revenue (assuming demand is inelastic).
    d. Because good weather increases the demand for, and price of, farm inputs.

6. Suppose there is a target price program. Under this program 500 bushels of X are produced at a target price of $7 per bushel but consumers will only buy 500 bushels at $4 per bushel. What is the total deficiency payment to farmerse?
    a. $1,500
    b. $2,000
    c. $3,000
    d. $1,000

7. Which agricultural policy results in the government buying and storing surplus production?
    a. acreage allotments
    b. target prices
    c. support prices
    d. marketing quotas
    e. production flexibility contracts

8. A price support is an example of a(an)
    a. price ceiling.
    b. price floor.
    c. acreage allotment.
    d. marketing quota.
    e. b and d

9. In 2002, the federal government replaced production flexibility contract payments with fixed direct payments, which essentially work the same way as production flexibility contract payments. The payment (under production flexibility contraction payments) is equal to
    a. Contract acreage x 0.95 x Yield per acre.
    b. Contract acreage x 0.85 x Yield per acre x Crop payment rate.
    c. Crop payment rate x 0.54 x Yield per acre.
    d. Yield per acre x Crop payment rate.
    e. none of the above

10. To obtain a nonrecourse loan, a farmer
    a. pledges a quantity of a commodity.
    b. puts a certain quantity of a commodity into storage.
    c. takes a certain number of acres out of rotation.
    d. b or c
    e. none of the above

True-False
Write "T" or "F" after each statement.

11. Bad weather may be good for farmers (in that farmers may earn more income with bad weather than good weather). _____

12. If market demand is inelastic and supply is subject to serve shifts from season to season, it follows that price changes are likely to be small. _____

13. The U.S. Congress passes a farm bill about every five years. _____

14. The greater the gap between the target price and the market price the greater the deficiency payment.

    _____

15. A nonrecourse loan is a particular type of counter-cyclical payment. _____

Fill in the Blank
Write the correct word in the blank.

16. The demand for many agricultural products is _____, which means if price falls, total revenue _____.

17. _____ _____ _____ _____ refers to the responsiveness of a change in quantity demanded to a change in income.

18. An agricultural price support is an example of a _____ _____.

19. Under a price support program, consumers end up paying _____ _____.

20. In 2004, farm households (in the United States) earned about _____ percent more than the U.S. average household income.

Answer Key

Chapter 1
Answers

Review Questions

1. Yes and no. This is only part of scarcity. Scarcity is the condition in which people have infinite wants *and* there are not enough resources (finite resources) to satisfy those wants.
2. A good gives a person utility or satisfaction; a bad gives a person disutility or dissatisfaction. People want goods and they don't want bads.
3. Josie likes to play music on Friday night. Music is a good on Friday night. Josie doesn't like to play music when she is studying for an exam. At that time, music is a bad.
4. The opportunity cost of your reading this study guide is whatever you would be doing if you weren't reading it. If you would be watching television, then watching television is the opportunity cost of your reading this study guide.
5. People are interested in only doing things when the benefits are greater than the costs. As the cost of smoking rises, it will be the case (for some people) that the benefits of smoking will no longer be greater than the costs, and therefore they will quit smoking.
6. marginal
7. Harriet considers what is relevant. Only the benefits of the next hour and the costs of the next hour are relevant to her. Costs and benefits in the past are not relevant. What does it matter what the costs and benefits have been? What matters is what they are expected to be. Marginal benefits and marginal costs deal with "additions," hence they deal with benefits and costs to come.
8. Answers will vary. Here is a sample answer. Someone takes a sleeping pill at night in order to get a restful sleep. Getting a restful sleep is the intended effect. The person does get a restful sleep, but also feels rather groggy for the first two hours she is up in the morning. Feeling groggy is an unintended effect.
9. Because scarcity exists—because our wants are greater than the resources available to satisfy them— we must decide (choose) which of our wants we will satisfy and which of our wants we won't satisfy. When we make choices, we necessarily incur an opportunity cost. After all, to choose to do X is to choose not to do Y. Y is the opportunity cost of doing X.
10. To think in terms of what would have been is to think in terms of opportunity cost. For example, you choose to go for a jog by the beach. What might have been had you not decided to jog by the beach? What would you have done instead? Whatever it was, it was the opportunity cost of your jogging by the beach.
11. The right amount of time to study—or the efficient amount of time to study—is the amount of time at which the marginal benefits of studying equal the marginal costs.
12. Land, labor, capital, and entrepreneurship.
13. To make themselves better off.
14. Because bads give people disutility and goods give people utility. People always want more utility and less disutility.
15. It means that he or she has exercised until the marginal benefits of exercising equal the marginal costs of exercising.
16. Price is being used as a rationing device. Having to use a rationing device is a consequence of scarcity. Another economic concept might be choice, in that Jim has to choose between goods he can buy.
17. It means that everything comes with an opportunity cost.
18. Saying there are no $10 bills on the sidewalk is the same as saying no one leaves net benefits on the sidewalk; instead, people try to maximize net benefits.
19. Microeconomics deals with the individual, the firm, a particular market. It deals with the small in economics such as the price of a good, the output produced by a single firm, etc. Macroeconomics deals with the big – the economy, the unemployment rate, the price level, etc.
20. Normative economics deals with *what should be*; positive economics deals with *what is*.

Problems

1.

```
┌─────────────┐        ┌─────────────┐
│   Scarcity  │───────▶│   Choice    │
└─────────────┘        └─────────────┘
                              │
                              ▼
                       ┌─────────────┐
                       │ Opportunity │
                       │    Cost     │
                       └─────────────┘
```

2.

Factor	Benefits of attending college	Costs of attending college	More likely to go to college? Yes or No
Jim thought he would earn $20 an hour if he didn't go to college, but learns that he will earn $35 an hour instead.		↑	No
His friends are going to college and he likes being around his friends.	↑		Yes
The salary gap between college graduates and high school graduates has widened.	↑		Yes
Jim learns something about himself: he doesn't like to study.		↑	No
The college he is thinking about attending just opened a satellite campus near Jim's home.		↓	Yes
The economy has taken a downturn and it looks like there are very few jobs for high school graduates right now.		↓	Yes

3. a. microeconomics, b. macroeconomics, c. macroeconomics, d. macroeconomics, e. microeconomics, f. microeconomics, g. microeconomics

4. Answers will vary. In each case, you want to ask yourself what you would do if you chose not to do the activity specified. The following are some sample answers.

Activity	Opportunity Cost
Study one more hour each night	Watch television
Take a long trip to someplace you have always wanted to visit	Buy a new car
Sit in the back of the room in one of your classes	Sit in the middle of the room
Talk up more in class	Daydream
Get a regular medical checkup	Play tennis
Surf the Web more	Watch television

What Is Wrong?

1. People have finite wants and infinite resources.

    People have infinite wants and resources are finite. This is scarcity.

2. People prefer more bads to fewer bads.

    Since people receive disutility from bads, they want fewer bads. Alternatively, you could say that people prefer more goods to fewer goods.

3. Scarcity is an effect of competition.

    Competition is an effect of scarcity.

4. The lower the opportunity cost of playing tennis, the less likely a person will play tennis.

    The lower the opportunity cost of playing tennis, the more likely a person will play tennis. The higher the opportunity cost of playing tennis, the less likely a person will play tennis.

5. Microeconomics is the branch of economics that deals with human behavior and choices as they relate to highly aggregate markets or the entire economy.

    Macroeconomics is the branch of economics that deals with human behavior and choices as they relate to highly aggregate markets or the entire economy.

6. Positive economics is to normative economics what opinion is to truth.

    Positive economics and truth are more closely aligned, as are normative economics and opinion.

7. Because there are rationing devices, there will always be scarcity.

    Because there is scarcity, there will always be rationing devices.

8. The four factors of production, or resources, are land, labor, capital, and profit.

    Profit is not a factor of production, it is a payment to a factor of production. The missing factor of production is entrepreneurship.

9. In a two-person exchange, one person is made better off while the other person is made worse off.

    In a two-person exchange, both persons are made better off.

10. If X is a good for Smith, it must then be a good for Jones too.

    If X is a good for Smith, it does not necessarily follow that X is good for Jones too.

Multiple Choice

1. c
2. b
3. a
4. b
5. c
6. c
7. a
8. c
9. c
10. d

True-False

11. T
12. F
13. T
14. F
15. F

Fill in the Blank

16. Macroeconomics
17. marginal
18. capital
19. entrepreneur
20. Exchange

Chapter 2
Answers

Review Questions

1. *Ex ante* position. *Ex ante* means before the exchange.
2. Economic growth is represented as a shift rightward in the PPF.
3. Choice is represented by any point on or below the PPF. Opportunity cost is (best) represented as a movement from one point on the PPF to another point on the PPF.
4. It means consumers prefer low to high prices for what they buy.
5. The transaction costs of buying a hamburger are lower than selling a house. There are many things involved in selling a house—finding an agent to list the house, signing contracts, etc.
6. Jake buys a cigarette from George and then smokes the cigarette while sitting next to Tabitha. Tabitha is allergic to cigarette smoke.
7. $1X = 1.5Y$; $1Y = 0.66X$
8. Through specialization and trade people can consume more goods. But this doesn't answer why this happens. It happens because when people specialize, they produce those things that they can produce at a lower cost than other people. In other words, they are doing what they do best and then trading with others. If everyone does what he or she does best, you would naturally think that everyone has to be better off—at least as compared to the situation where no one does his or her best.
9. People trade to make themselves better off. The necessary condition: People have to value what they will trade for more than what they will trade with. For example, if Yvonne trades $10 for a book, she values the book (which she doesn't currently have) more than the $10 (which she currently does have).
10. We have to give up 10 units of X to produce the first 10 units of Y, but we have to give up 20 units of X to produce the second 10 units of Y.
11. It indicates constant costs.
12. It indicates increasing costs.
13. These are two points *on* its PPF, which means the two points are efficient. Efficiency implies the impossibility of gains in one area without losses in another. This is what a tradeoff is about: more of one thing, but less of something else.
14. An advance in technology; more resources.
15. Answers will vary. The example you come up with should make it possible to produce more goods with the same resources.
16. In the example in the chapter, an entrepreneur sees that there is profit by taking a potential exchange (between two individuals) and turning it into an actual exchange. He acts accordingly.

Problems

1. 1 hat = $30 or 1 hat = $20. Any price lower than $40 gives us the correct answer.
2. If the entrepreneur can lower Karen's transaction costs from $60 to $24 (a reduction of $36), then Karen will make the trade. Karen will think this way: I pay $370 to the seller, and $5 to the entrepreneur, for a total of $375. My maximum buying price is $400, so I will receive $25 net benefit. But what about transaction costs? As long as my transaction costs are not more than, say, $24, I will receive at least $1 net benefit and the exchange is worth it to me. The entrepreneur will have to lower Randy's transaction costs from $60 to $14 (a reduction of $46). Randy will think this way: I receive $370 from the buyer and I pay $5 to the entrepreneur. This leaves me with $365. My minimum selling price is $350, so I receive $15 net benefit. But what about transaction costs? As long as my transaction costs are not higher than, say, $14, I will receive $1 net benefit and the exchange is worth it to me.

3.

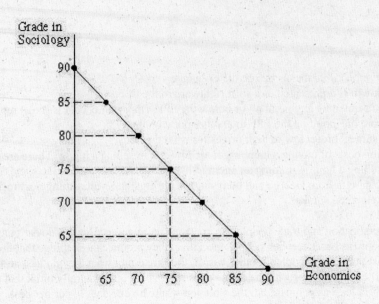

4.   5 fewer points in sociology.
5.   Points A and D
6.   Points B and C
7.   Points E and F
8.   Yes, point D could be efficient. The reason why is that there are tradeoffs moving from one efficient point to another. In other words, more of one good comes with less of another good.
9.

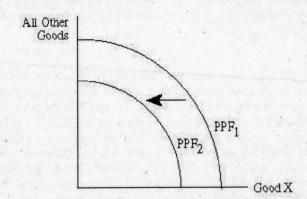

10.

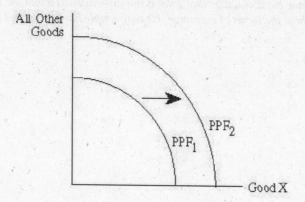

What Is Wrong?

1. If costs are increasing, the PPF is a straight (downward-sloping) line.

    If costs are increasing, the PPF is bowed outward. Alternatively you could say: If costs are constant, the PPF is a straight line.

2. If Jones can produce either (a) 100 units of X and 100 units of Y or (b) 200 units of X and zero units of Y, then he has a comparative advantage in the production of Y.

    We don't know whether he has a comparative advantage in Y or not. To know this, we have to compare his costs to someone else's costs.

3. The following PPF represents a 2-for-1 opportunity cost of apples.

    It is a 1-for-1 opportunity cost of apples. For every apple produced, one orange is not produced. For every one orange produced, one apple is not produced.

4. There are probably more unemployed resources at point A than at point D.

    There are more unemployed resources at D, a point below the PPF.

5. Efficiency implies the possibility of gains in one area without losses in another area.

    Efficiency implies the impossibility of gains in one area without losses in another area. Alternatively, you could have written, Inefficiency implies the possibility of gains in one area without losses in another area.

6. If Georgina reads one more book, she will have to give up doing something else. This shows that Georgina is inefficient.

    When there is efficiency, there are tradeoffs. Georgina cannot do more of one thing without doing less of something else.

7. If Bobby can produce either (a) 100 units of good X and 50 units of good Y, or (b) 25 units of good X and 80 units of good Y, then the cost of 1 unit of good X is 1.5 units of good Y.

    The cost of 1 unit of good X is 0.4 units of good Y.

8. John says, "I bought this sweater yesterday and I think I got a bad deal." It follows that in the *ex ante* position John thought he would be better off with the sweater than with the money he paid for it, but in the *ex post* position he prefers the money to the sweater.

This could be true, but it could be that John is not disheartened about the trade (of money for the sweater), but about the terms of exchange. He may simply have preferred to pay less for the sweater.

Multiple Choice
1. b
2. d
3. c
4. c
5. c
6. e
7. a
8. d
9. b
10. a
11. e
12. d
13. e

True-False
14. T
15. F
16. F
17. T
18. T

Fill in the Blank
19. Inefficiency
20. Efficiency
21. 8
22. transaction costs
23. opportunity costs
24. efficient
25. straight line

Chapter 3
Answers

Review Questions

1. Price and quantity demanded are inversely related, *ceteris paribus*.
2. Price and quantity demanded move in opposite directions: as price rises, quantity demanded falls, and as price falls, quantity demanded rises.
3. Amount of a good buyers are willing and able to buy at a particular price. For example, quantity demanded may be 100 units at $10 per unit.
4. Quantity demanded is a specific number—such as 100 units. Demand is a relationship between various prices and various quantities demanded.
5. income, preferences, prices of related goods (substitutes and complements), number of buyers, expectations of future price.
6. to the right
7. to the left
8. Amount of a good sellers are willing and able to produce at a particular price.
9. Quantity supplied is constant as price changes. Stated differently, quantity supplied is independent of (does not depend on) changes in price.
10. Price and quantity supplied are directly related.
11. prices of relevant resources, technology, number of sellers, expectations of future price, taxes and subsidies, government restrictions
12. to the right
13. to the left
14. Quantity of the good is on the horizontal axis, price is on the vertical axis.
15. The absolute price of a good is the money price of a good—such as $3,000 for a computer. The relative price of a good is the price of the good in terms of some other good. For example, if the absolute price of a computer is $3,000, and the absolute price of a TV set is $1,000, then the relative price of a computer (in terms of TV sets) is 3 TV sets.
16. Equilibrium price and quantity rise.
17. Equilibrium price falls and equilibrium quantity rises.
18. Equilibrium price and quantity rise.
19. Equilibrium price rises and equilibrium quantity falls.
20. Consumers' surplus falls. Consumers' surplus equals maximum buying price minus price paid, so if price paid rises, consumers' surplus must fall.

Problems
1.

Factor	Demand	Supply	Equilibrium Price	Equilibrium Quantity
Price of a substitute rises	↑		↑	↑
Price of a complement falls	↑		↑	↑
Income rises (normal good)	↑		↑	↑
Income falls (inferior good)	↑		↑	↑
Price of relevant resource rises		↓	↑	↓
Technology advances		↑	↓	↑
Quota		↓	↑	↓
Number of buyers rises	↑		↑	↑
Number of sellers rises		↑	↓	↑
Buyers expect higher price	↑		↑	↑
Sellers expect higher price		↓	↑	↓
Tax on production		↓	↑	↓
Preferences become more favorable with respect to the good	↑		↑	↑

2.

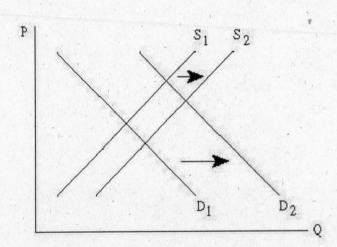

3.

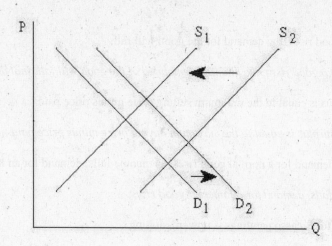

4. A + B + C + D
5. E + F + G + H
6. 140 − 50 = 90 units
7. 180 − 60 = 120 units
8.

Price	Quantity demanded by John	Quantity demanded by Mary	Quantity demanded (market demand)
$10	100	130	230
$12	80	120	200
$14	50	100	150

9. $6
10. Jack's first candy bar gives him more utility than the second; the second gives him more utility than the third; and so on.

What Is Wrong?

1. If the price of a good rises, the demand for the good will fall.

    If the price of a good rises, the quantity demanded of the good will fall. (not demanded)

2. Consumers' surplus is equal to the minimum selling price minus price paid.

    Consumers' surplus is equal to the maximum buying price minus price paid.

3. As income rises, demand for a normal good rises; as income falls, demand for an inferior good falls.

    …as income falls, demand for an inferior good rises.

4. The supply curve for Picasso paintings is upward-sloping.

    The supply curve for Picasso paintings is vertical.

5. As price rises, supply rises; as price falls, supply falls.

    As price rises, quantity supplied rises; as price falls, quantity supplied falls.

6. Quantity demanded is greater than supply when there is a shortage.

    Quantity demanded is greater than quantity supplied when there is a shortage.

7. If supply rises, and demand is constant, equilibrium price rises and equilibrium quantity rises.

    If supply rises, and demand is constant, equilibrium price falls and equilibrium quantity rises.

8. The law of diminishing marginal utility states that as a consumer consumes additional units of a good, each successive unit gives him or her more utility than the previous unit.

    …each successive unit gives him or her less utility than the previous unit.

9. According to the law of demand, as the price of a good rises, the quantity demanded of the good rises, *ceteris paribus.*

    According to the law of demand, as the price of a good rises, the quantity demanded of the good falls, ceteris paribus.

Multiple Choice
1. d
2. c
3. e
4. b
5. c
6. b
7. b
8. b
9. e
10. b
11. d
12. a
13. a
14. d
15. d

True-False
16. F
17. F
18. T
19. F
20. T

Fill in the Blank
21. falls; rises
22. market
23. inferior
24. increases
25. equals
26. tie-in

Chapter 4
Answers

Review Questions

1. Requirements for admission (scores on standardized tests, grade point averages) will rise. As student tuition remains constant in the face of rising demand, the gap between the student tuition and equilibrium tuition will increase. Or, the shortage of spaces at the university will increase. There will be "more work" for the nonprice rationing devices to do.

2. Here is an example to illustrate our answer. A person pays $2,000 a year in health insurance. After making the payment, the only dollar cost for medical care the person has to concern herself with is her co-payment or deductible. Let's say her co-payment is $5 and her deductible is $200. Now think of a situation where the person has already met her deductible. The price of medical care is, say, only $5 per physician or hospital visit. At this low price, we would expect the quantity demanded of medical care to be high. A high "quantity demanded of medical care" translates into a high demand for certain medical procedures. In the text, we talked about the demand for X-rays (as the medical procedure). High demand for these medical procedures ends up raising the price of these procedures.

3. By price.

4. The supply curve (of housing) is steeper in region 1 than 2.

5. If the university charges a below-equilibrium price for parking, there will be a shortage of parking spaces. Something will have to ration the available parking spots. It is more likely to be first-come-first-served (FCFS). What happens if you're not one of the first in line to park? You might end up being late to class.

6. Raise price, raise supply, lower demand. The freeway congestion is evidence of a shortage. There are three ways to get rid of a shortage. The first is to allow price to move up to its equilibrium level, where quantity demanded is equal to quantity supplied. The second is to raise supply enough so that there is no more shortage. The third is to lower demand enough so that there is no more shortage. Increasing supply, in the context of freeway congestion, means adding more freeways. Lowering demand means, perhaps, giving people an incentive to carpool to a greater degree.

7. The price floor or ceiling might make them better off (although it might make others worse off).

8. Yes, patients will pay more for health care when they have the right to sue their provider than when they do not have the right to sue. That's because when patients have the right to sue, the costs to the provider of providing health care are higher, and thus the supply curve of health care is closer to the origin. This results in a higher price for health care.

9. The price (people pay) for good weather is one component of the overall price for housing in a good-weather city.

10. College classes are not usually "sold" at equilibrium prices. The price (tuition) charged for one class might be below equilibrium, so that a shortage of that class exists.

Problems

1. Suppose there is a downward-sloping demand for losing one's temper. If so, the higher the price to lose one's temper, the less one will lose one's temper. Yvonne's father charges her a higher price to lose her temper than Yvonne's mother charges her. Notice that people don't often lose their tempers with their bosses (the price you would have to pay is too high), but will lose their tempers with family members, etc.

2. Driving takes time. For example, it might take 20 minutes, going at 50 mph, to go from point X to point Y. The more valuable time is, the more a person will want to economize on time. How valuable time is may be a function of one's wage rate. The higher one's wage rate, the more valuable time is, and the more one will want to economize on time. The 68-year-old retired person may face a lower wage rate than the 32-year-old working person and so time is less valuable to the older person than to the younger person. We would expect the 68-year-old to care less about whether or not he drives slowly because time is less valuable to him or her.

3. Answers will vary. Here is a sample answer. When students pay the equilibrium, professors know that the quantity demanded of spots at the university equals the quantity supplied. If they do something that students don't like, then the demand curve may fall (for education at the university) and, at the given tuition, quantity supplied will be greater than quantity demanded. In other words, there will be a surplus. Will the university get rid of some professors when this happens? Now consider the case when students pay below-equilibrium tuition. Professors know that there is a shortage of space at the university. If they do something that some of their students don't like, and the students leave the university, there are others to take their places (because of the shortage). We predict the following. *If there is a difference between the way a professor wants to teach a class and the way students want it taught, the professor is more likely to respond to the preferences of the students in the first setting (where students pay equilibrium tuition) than in the second setting (where there is a shortage of students due to a below-equilibrium tuition being charged).*

4. Answers will vary. This is a good question to think about.

5. After decriminalization, the demand for marijuana increases by the same amount as the supply of marijuana.

6. Both believe there will be a cutback in employment, so there is no disagreement as to direction (down). The argument is over the magnitude of the downward change.

7. It must be vertical. The supply curve of kidneys discussed in the text was upward-sloping, not vertical. An upward-sloping supply curve illustrates a direct relationship between price and quantity supplied.

8. If a candy bar sells for more in location X than Y, candy bars will be moved from Y to X in search of the higher price. In other words, the supply of candy bars will be reallocated in such a way that no candy bar (in any location) will sell for more or less than any other candy bar. It is not as easy to reallocate houses on land. In short, if a house sells for more in location X than Y, it is difficult (if not impossible) to pick up the house (attached to the land it is on) and move it from Y to X. Since the supply of houses on land cannot be reallocated as easily as candy bars, we would expect that housing prices may differ between locations whereas candy bar prices will not.

9. A car that does not sell does not mean "a bad car." It could simply mean a higher-than-equilibrium price. Jones's car may be a great car, for which the equilibrium price may be, say, $30,000. However, if Jones is charging $100,000 for the car, no one will buy it.

10. He or she forgets, overlooks, or ignores that professors in different fields do not all face the same market conditions. The demand for economists may be higher than the demand for sociologists, and if the supply of each is the same, the equilibrium wage for economists will be higher than the equilibrium wage for sociologists. Suppose we pay economists the same as sociologists, and that the salary we pay each is midway between the equilibrium wage of economists and the equilibrium wage of sociologists. What happens now? There will be a shortage of economists and a surplus of sociologists.

What May Have Been Overlooked?

1. The higher the demand for something, the greater the quantity demanded.

    This is true at a given price. However, a lower price and lower demand can generate a greater quantity demanded than a higher price and higher demand.

2. I think how I behave is independent of the setting that I am in. I act the same way no matter what the setting.

    The person has overlooked the fact that the price of acting a certain way may be different in different settings and that people usually respond to changes in price.

3. If house prices rise by 10 percent in city A, then they will probably rise by the same percentage in city B.

    Demand may not have increased by the same percentage in each city or supply might not have fallen by the same percentage in each city. Or, even if demand increased by the same in each city, the steepness of the supply curve in each city might have been different.

4. The rock bank has the best interest of its fans in mind. It knows it can charge $80 a ticket, but it charges only $20 a ticket so that its fans won't have to pay so much.

    What the rock band forgets is that people pay in money or in something else. If $80 is the equilibrium price, then $20 is a below-equilibrium price, at which there will be a shortage of tickets. How will the tickets be rationed? By a combination of first-come-first-served (FCFS). FCFS will no doubt lead to fans standing in long lines to get tickets, some of whom will end up not getting the tickets. Fans will pay by standing in line instead of more money.

5. If my university doesn't charge for student parking, then I am definitely better off than I would be if it did charge for student parking.

    Not necessarily. If there is some positive equilibrium price for parking, then a zero price will create a shortage of parking spots and some nonprice rationing device will come into play. It will probably be first-come-first-served (FCFS), which will cause students to have to pay for parking spots in time instead of money.

6. The tuition at Harvard is very high, so Harvard must be charging the equilibrium tuition to students. Still, Harvard uses such things as GPA, SAT and ACT scores for admission purposes. It must be wrong that these nonprice rationing devices (GPA, etc.) are used only by colleges and universities that charge below-equilibrium tuition.

    The demand for Harvard may be very high, such that even at the high tuition charged, there still is a shortage of spots at Harvard. In other words, Harvard can still charge a high tuition and the high tuition may still not be high enough to equal the equilibrium tuition.

7. If a good doesn't have a money price, it has no price at all.

    Price connotes sacrifice, or giving up something to get something. Someone offers you free tickets to a concert if you will drive to his house and pick up the tickets and later that week mow his lawn. No money has changed hands, but if you accept the deal you will have to pay a nonmoney price for the tickets.

Multiple Choice

1. e
2. b
3. b
4. b
5. a
6. c
7. b
8. a
9. b
10. e
11. e
12. a
13. b
14. b
15. d

True-False
16. T
17. T
18. T
19. F
20. F (the higher the price of medical care, the lower the quantity demanded of medical care)

Fill in the Blank
21. quantity demanded
22. higher
23. nonprice rationing
24. consumers' surplus
25. John's; Bill

Chapter 5
Answers

Review Questions
1. Economists use a price index to measure the price level.
2. No, the CPI is not a reflection of the prices of all goods and services in the economy—only those that are in the market basket.
3. First, it means that prices in this year are higher than in the base year (whatever year that happens to be) because the CPI in the base year is always 100. By itself, the CPI of 132 doesn't mean much more. It is only when we compare the CPI of 132 to other things that we derive some meaning. For example, if the CPI is 120 in the year before, then using the CPI of 132, we can compute how much prices (on average) have risen over the year.
4. We compute real income by (1) dividing nominal income by the CPI and then (2) multiplying by 100. Two people may have the same nominal income, but if they live in different countries, and face different CPIs, then they will have different real incomes. For example, $40,000 in a country where prices are low goes much further than $40,000 in a country where prices are high.
5. $40,000 in 1987 was not the same (in terms of purchasing power) as $40,000 in 2003, unless prices were the same in 1987 as in 2003, which they weren't.
6. There are a number of steps to calculating the CPI: (1) define the market basket; (2) identify current-year prices and base-year prices; (3) use the market basket and current-year prices to determine the total expenditure on the market basket in the current year; (4) use the market basket and base-year prices to determine the total expenditure on the market basket in the base year; (5) divide the total expenditure on the market basket in the current year by the total expenditure on the market basket in the base year; and (6) multiply by 100.
7. The civilian noninstitutional population is a larger number than the civilian labor force because the civilian labor force is a subset of the noninstitutional population. The civilian noninstitutional population is equal to the persons not in the labor force plus the persons in the civilian labor force. The civilian labor force is equal to the number of employed persons plus the number of unemployed persons. Look at it this way. Everyone in the civilian labor force is in the civilian noninstitutional population, but not everyone in the civilian noninstitutional population is in the civilian labor force. Who isn't? Obviously, the persons not in the labor force.
8. No. The employment rate and the unemployment rate have different denominators, and so therefore do not have to add up to 100 percent. The denominator of the employment rate is the civilian noninstitutional population. The denominator of the unemployment rate is the civilian labor force.
9. Job leaver, job loser, reentrant, entrant.
10. A reentrant was previously employed full time, an entrant was not.
11. They do not meet any of the conditions specified in question number 8 above.
12. Mary works as an accountant. The demand for accounting services falls and Mary loses her job. No accountants are currently being hired. The only businesses that are hiring are those that are looking for computer analysts. Mary doesn't currently have the skills to be a computer analyst. Mary is structurally unemployed.

Problems
1. Multiply current-year prices by the market basket to find the total expenditure on the market basket in the current year. This is $150.95. Then multiply base-year prices by the market basket to find the total expenditure on the market basket in the base year. This is $112.55. Next divide the total expenditure on the market basket in the current year by the total expenditure on the market basket in the base year. This gives us 1.34. Finally, multiply by 100 to get the CPI of 134.

2.

$$\left(\frac{177.1 - 140.3}{140.3} \right) \times 100 = 26.2\%$$

3. Real income is $34,965.
4. Yes, Rebecca's real income did rise since her nominal income increased by a greater percentage than prices increased.
5. $10,000 in 1967 was equivalent to $53,023 in 2001. To get the answer: (a) divide the CPI in 2001 by the CPI in 1967; (b) multiply the outcome of (a) by 10,000.
6.

Category	Number of persons
Civilian noninstitutional population	200
Employed	100
Civilian labor force	120
Unemployment rate	16.67 percent
Persons unemployed	20
Persons not in the labor force	80

7. 200/280 = 71.42 percent
8. The labor force participation rate is the civilian labor force as a percentage of the civilian noninstitutional population. The employment rate is the number of employed persons as a percentage of the civilian noninstitutional population.
9. No, we would also need to know the number of entrants. Unemployed persons = job losers + job leavers + reentrants + entrants.
10. No, because to compute the cyclical unemployment rate, we also need to know the actual unemployment rate in the economy.

What Is the Question?

1. The consumer price index.

   What is one price index used to measure the price level?

2. Take the nominal income and divide it by the CPI. Then take the quotient and multiply it by 100.

   How do you compute real income?

3. The number of persons employed plus the number of persons unemployed.

   What does the civilian labor force equal?

4. The natural unemployment rate minus the frictional unemployment rate.

   What does the structural unemployment rate equal?

5. This person is not considered unemployed (by the government), even though many people think this person should be considered unemployed.

   What is a discouraged worker?

6. The cyclical unemployment rate.

   What do you call the difference between the actual unemployment rate in the economy and the natural unemployment rate?

7. The first step is to subtract the CPI in the earlier year from the CPI in the later year. The second step is to divide by the CPI in the earlier year. The third step is to multiply by 100.

   How do you compute the percentage change in prices (using the CPI)?

8. This happens if the CPI rises by more than your nominal income.

   What happens when real income falls?

9. This person did at least one hour of work as a paid employee during the survey week.

   What is an employed person?

10. This person quit his job.

    What is a job leaver?

11. This person got fired but doesn't (currently) have transferable skills.

    What is a job loser who is structurally unemployed?

Multiple Choice
1. c
2. c
3. c
4. d
5. a
6. e
7. d
8. e
9. c
10. b
11. b
12. d
13. b
14. d
15. a

True-False
16. F
17. T
18. T
19. T
20. T

Fill in the Blank
21. unemployment rate
22. price index
23. real income
24. natural unemployment
25. base year

Chapter 6
Answers

Review Questions
1. Total market value refers to the monetary value of something at today's prices. For example, suppose two units of good X are sold (today) for $50 per unit. Total market value of these two goods is $100.
2. A hamburger at a fast food restaurant is a final good. The lettuce on the hamburger is an intermediate good.
3. GDP only measures current production. Sales of used goods do not deal with current production. A used good is a good produced in the past that is sold today.
4. GDP measures production. A financial transaction does not deal with production. A financial transaction, such as a purchase of 100 shares of stock, deals with a change in ownership rights. When John buys 100 shares of stock from Taylor, there is no production involved. John simply owns what Taylor used to own.
5. Durable goods, nondurable goods, and services.
6. Fixed investment is the sum of the purchases of new capital goods and the purchases of new residential housing.
7. GDP measures production. Transfer payments have nothing to do with production. A transfer payment is a payment to a person that is not made in return for goods and services currently supplied (produced).
8. National income is equal to compensation of employees plus proprietors' income plus corporate profits plus rental income plus net interest.
9. GDP minus the capital consumption allowance.
10. Personal income is the income that people actually receive. There is some component of national income that is earned but not received (such as corporate profits taxes) and some part of national income that is received but not earned (such as transfer payments). You may want to think of national income as income earned, and personal income as income received.
11. Disposable income is personal income minus personal taxes.
12. No; it is possible for GDP to rise and Real GDP to remain unchanged. GDP is equal to prices multiplied by output. Real GDP is simply output (in base year prices). It is possible for prices to rise, the level of output to stay the same, and therefore GDP will rise. Real GDP will not change, though.
13. Economic growth is the percentage change in Real GDP.

Problems
1. Only the $23 price goes into the computation of GDP. GDP measures the total market value of *final goods and services…*
2. GDP equals $100. Everything except Carl's production is not included in GDP.
3. Yes, since the purchases of new residential housing is a component of fixed investment.
4. $C + I + G + (EX - IM)$
5. A fall in output or a fall in prices. Think of GDP as being equal to current-year prices multiplied by current-year quantity. If either prices or quantities fall, so does GDP.
6. Some of the items in the table are not relevant to computing GDP. GDP = $C + I + G + (EX - IM)$. Consumption is the sum of durable goods, nondurable goods, and services. Investment is given. Government purchases is the sum of purchases by all levels of government—federal, state, and local. Exports is given, as is imports. GDP is equal to $1,125 million.
7. Some of the items in the table are not relevant to computing national income. National income is the sum of compensation of employees, proprietors' income, corporate profits, rental income, and net interest. National income is equal to $1,060 million.
8. Some of the items in the table are not relevant to computing personal income. Personal income is equal to national income minus undistributed corporate profits minus social insurance taxes minus corporate profits taxes plus transfer payments. Personal income is equal to $900 million.

9. GDP is equal to the sum of current-year quantities multiplied by current-year prices. GDP = $2,600. Real GDP is equal to the sum of current-year quantities multiplied by base-year prices. Real GDP = $1,200.

10. To find per capita GDP, simply divide GDP by population.

GDP	Population	Per capita GDP
$1,200 billion	100 million	$12,000
$500 billion	67 million	$7,462
$3,000 billion	50 million	$60,000

11. GNP is equal to GDP minus income earned by the rest of the world plus income earned from the rest of the world. Here's the explanation of how we get this equation. U.S. GDP, we know, includes the income a noncitizen (who lives in the U.S.) earns. This income a noncitizen earns is called "income earned by the rest of the world." First, subtract this amount from GDP. Then to turn what we have left into GNP, we have to add the income a U.S. citizen earns in another country. This we call "income earned from the rest of the world." So, GNP is equal to GDP minus income earned by the rest of the world plus income earned from the rest of the world.

12. GDP is equal to GNP minus income earned from the rest of the world plus income earned by the rest of the world. Here's the explanation of how we get this equation. We know that GNP contains the income a U.S. citizens earns in another country. This income is called "income earned from the rest of the world." First, subtract this amount GNP. Then take what we are left with and add income earned by the rest of the world to get GDP. In other words, GDP is equal to GNP minus income earned from the rest of the world plus income earned by the rest of the world.

13. Yes, since we know that NDP is equal to GDP minus capital consumption allowance, it follows that GDP is equal to NDP plus capital consumption allowance.

14. No, there is a contraction, recovery, and expansion between one peak and the next. Knowing that peak to peak is March to July doesn't give us any information on how long the contraction is, or how long the recovery is, or how long the expansion is. If we knew the length of peak to peak, and knew the length of the contraction, and the length of the recovery, we could then figure out the length of the expansion.

15. 12 + 13 + 12 = 37 months.

What Is Wrong?

1. The expansion phase of a business cycle is generally longer than the recovery stage.

   There is no telling how long each stage will be.

2. A stock variable makes little sense without some time period specified.

   A flow variable makes little sense without some time period specified. Alternatively, you could write, A stock variable makes sense without some time period specified.

3. Fixed investment includes business purchases of new capital goods, inventory investment, and purchases of new residential housing.

   Fixed investment includes only business purchases of new capital goods and purchases of new residential housing.

4. GDP = C + I + G + EX + IM

   $GDP = C + I + G + EX - IM$

5. Net domestic product is equal to GDP minus capital consumption allowance. Another name for capital consumption allowance is capital good.

    Another name for the capital consumption allowance is depreciation.

6. A business cycle is measured from trough to peak.

    A business cycle is measured from peak to peak.

7. The largest expenditure component of GDP is government purchases.

    The largest expenditure component of GDP is consumption.

What Is the Question?

1. GDP divided by population.

    What is per capita GDP equal to?

2. Five phases: peak, contraction, trough, recovery, and expansion.

    How many phases are there in a business cycle and what are the phases?

3. First, subtract Real GDP in the earlier year from Real GDP in the current year. Second, divide by Real GDP in the earlier year. Third, multiply by 100.

    How do you compute the economic growth rate?

4. National income minus undistributed corporate profits minus social insurance taxes minus corporate profits taxes plus transfer payments.

    What is personal income equal to?

5. Personal income minus personal taxes.

    What is disposable income equal to?

Multiple Choice
1. a
2. b
3. e
4. e
5. e
6. c
7. c
8. d
9. e
10. e
11. e
12. a
13. e
14. b
15. a

True False
16. F
17. F
18. F
19. T
20. F

Fill in the Blank
21. two
22. five
23. trough
24. flow
25. Investment w

Chapter 7
Answers

Review Questions

1. According to economists, aggregate demand curves slope downward because of the (1) real-balance effect, (2) interest-rate effect, and (3) international-trade effect. The real-balance effect can be described as follows: As the price level rises, purchasing power falls, monetary wealth falls, and people end up buying fewer goods. As the price level falls, purchasing power rises, monetary wealth rises, and people end up buying more goods.

2. A change in the quantity demanded of Real GDP is a movement from one point to another point on a given AD curve. It is caused by a change in the price level. A change in aggregate demand refers to a rightward shift or leftward shift in the entire AD curve. It can be brought about by a change in consumption, government purchases, investment, and so on. A change in AD is representative of a change in the quantity demanded of Real GDP at a given price level.

3. Consumption, investment, government purchases, exports, and imports.

4. No, a lower price level will change the quantity demanded of Real GDP, it will not change AD.

5. wealth, expected future prices and income, interest rate, income taxes

6. interest rate, expected future sales, business taxes

7. real foreign national income, exchange rate

8. (1) Firms agree to a certain nominal wage for a specified period of time, (2) the price level falls, (3) as a result of a fall in the price level, the real wage rises, (4) firms hire fewer workers at higher real wages, (5) because fewer people are working, firms produce less output. Notice that a lower price level has led to less output. This gives us an upward-sloping SRAS curve.

9. (1) Both the price level and nominal wage fall by the same percentage, (2) the real wage does not change, (3) workers believe that the nominal wage has fallen by more than the price level and that their real wage has fallen, (4) in reaction to the "perceived" lower real wage, the quantity supplied of labor falls, (5) with less labor, firms produce less output. Notice that a lower price level has led to less output. This gives us an upward-sloping SRAS curve.

10. wage rates, prices of nonlabor inputs, productivity, supply shocks (adverse and beneficial)

Problems

1.

If...	AD curve shifts to the (right or left?)
consumption rises	right
investment rises	right
exports rise	right
imports rise	left
government purchases rise	right
consumption falls	left
net exports rise	right

2.

If...	SRAS curve shifts to the (right or left?)
wage rates rise	left
prices of nonlabor inputs fall	right
productivity increases	right
adverse supply shock	left
beneficial supply shock	right
wage rates fall	right

3.

Factor	How does the factor change affect C, I, G, EX, and/or IM?
wealth rises	C rises
individuals expect higher (future) prices	C rises
individuals expect higher (future) income	C rises
interest rate rises	C falls, I falls
income taxes fall	C rises
businesses expect higher (future) sales	I rises
business taxes rise	I falls
foreign real national income falls	EX falls
dollar appreciates	EX falls, IM rises
dollar depreciates	EX rises, IM falls

4.

Factor	Does the AD curve shift? (right, left, no change)	Does the SRAS curve shift? (right, left, no change)	Is there a change in the price level? (up, down, no change)	Is there a change in Real GDP? (up, down, no change)	Is there a change in the unemployment rate? (up, down, no change)
interest rate falls	right	no change	up	up	down
wage rates rise	no change	left	up	down	up
productivity rises	no change	right	down	up	down
adverse supply shock	no change	left	up	down	up
wealth falls	left	no change	down	down	up
businesses expect lower (future) sales	left	no change	down	down	up
dollar appreciates	left	no change	down	down	up
prices of nonlabor inputs rise	no change	left	up	down	up
beneficial supply shock	no change	right	down	up	down
wealth rises	right	no change	up	up	down
dollar depreciates	right	no change	up	up	down
wage rates fall	no change	right	down	up	down

5.

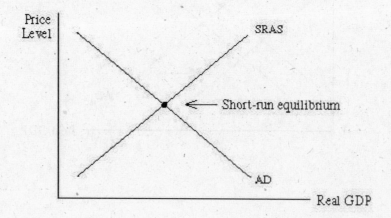

6.

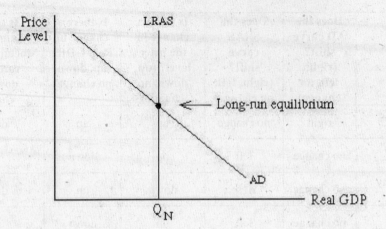

7.

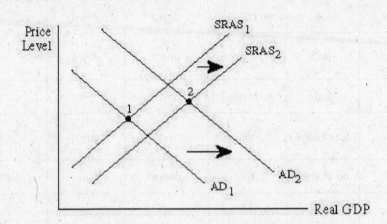

8.

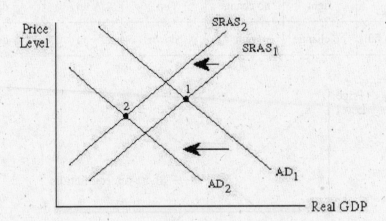

9.

Suppose…	Does the price level rise, fall, or remain constant?	Does Real GDP rise, fall, or remain constant?	Does the unemployment rate rise, fall, or remain constant?
AD rises	rise	rise	fall
AD rises by more than SRAS falls	rise	rise	fall
SRAS falls	rise	fall	rise
SRAS rises by the same amount as AD rises	remain constant	rise	fall
SRAS rises	fall	rise	fall
AD falls	fall	fall	rise

10. $225
11. £200

What Is Wrong?

1. Real GDP increased and the price level fell. This was because the AD curve shifted to the right.

   If the AD curve shifted to the right, the price level wouldn't fall. If the SRAS curve shifted to the right, Real GDP would rise and the price level would fall.

2. Real GDP and the price level increased. This was because the SRAS curve shifted to the right.

   If the SRAS curve shifted to the right, the price level would not increase. If the AD curve shifted to the right, Real GDP and the price level would increase.

3. If SRAS increases, the SRAS curve shifts upward and to the left.

   If SRAS increases, the SRAS curve shifts downward and to the right. Alternatively, you could write: If SRAS decreases, the SRAS curve shifts upward and to the left.

4. The price level increased and Real GDP decreased. This is because the AD curve shifted to the left.

   If the AD curve shifted to the left, the price level would not increase. If the SRAS curve shifts to the left, the price level would increase and Real GDP would decrease.

5. A change in interest rates will affect both consumption and government purchases.

   A change in interest rates will affect both consumption and investment.

6. If the dollar appreciates, this means it takes more dollars to buy a unit of foreign currency.

   If the dollar appreciates, this means it takes fewer dollars to buy a unit of foreign currency. Alternatively, you could write: If the dollar depreciates, this means it takes more dollars to buy a unit of foreign currency.

7. An increase in wealth will raise consumption, aggregate demand, and the price level. It will lower Real GDP.

   An increase in wealth will not lead to lower Real GDP, it will lead to higher Real GDP.

8. A decline in interest rates will raise consumption and investment, lower aggregate demand, shift the AD curve left, and raise the price level.

   A decline in interest rates will not lead to lower aggregate demand and to a leftward shift in the AD curve. It will lead to higher aggregate demand and a rightward shift in the AD curve.

9. The LRAS curve is vertical at the current level of Real GDP.

   The LRAS curve is vertical at the Natural Real GDP level.

10. Long-run equilibrium is at the intersection of the AD curve and the upward-sloping LRAS curve, while short-run equilibrium is at the intersection of the AD curve and the vertical SRAS curve.

    The LRAS curve is not upward sloping, it is vertical. The SRAS curve is not vertical, it is upward-sloping.

11. An increase in the interest rate will lower the demand for loanable funds.

    An increase in the interest rate will lower the quantity demanded of loanable funds.

Multiple Choice
1. b
2. a
3. c
4. c
5. c
6. d
7. d
8. b
9. c
10. c
11. c
12. d
13. b
14. a
15. e

True-False
16. T
17. F
18. T
19. T
20. F

Fill in the Blank
21. falls
22. rises
23. Productivity
24. AD
25. right

Chapter 8
Answers

Review Questions

1. Yes, according to classical economists, Say's law still holds. The savings simply lowers the interest rate and leads to a rise in investment. The rise in investment will be equal to the difference between income and consumption, or $100.
2. More saving leads to lower interest rates. Lower interest rates lead to more investment.
3. Classical economists believed that wages and prices were flexible. There are economists who believe this today.
4. The economy can remove itself from both inflationary and recessionary gaps.
5. The Real GDP that the economy is producing is less than Natural Real GDP.
6. The Real GDP that the economy is producing is greater than Natural Real GDP.
7. greater than
8. less than
9. surplus
10. shortage
11. The wage rate falls, the SRAS curve shifts to the right, and eventually intersects both the AD curve and LRAS curve at Natural Real GDP.
12. The wage rate rises, the SRAS curve shifts to the left, and eventually intersects both the AD curve and the LRAS curve at Natural Real GDP.

Problems
1.

State of the economy	The labor market is in (shortage, surplus, equilibrium)	The wage rate will (rise, fall, remain unchanged)	The SRAS curve will shift (right, left)
Recessionary gap	surplus	fall	right
Inflationary gap	shortage	rise	left
Long-run equilibrium	equilibrium	remain unchanged	remain unchanged

2. (b) the economy is removing itself from an inflationary gap. When the price level is falling, the SRAS curve is shifting to the right, which is what it does when the economy is removing itself from a recessionary gap. When it is removing itself from an inflationary gap, the SRAS curve is shifting to the left, and the price level is rising.
3. (b) the economy is removing itself from an inflationary gap. When Real GDP is rising, the SRAS curve is shifting to the right, which is what it does when the economy is removing itself from a recessionary gap. When it is removing itself from an inflationary gap, the SRAS curve is shifting to the left, and Real GDP is falling.
4. (a) the economy is removing itself from a recessionary gap. When Real GDP is rising, the SRAS curve is shifting to the right, which is what it does when the economy is removing itself from a recessionary gap.
5. (a) the economy is removing itself from a recessionary gap. When the price level is falling, the SRAS curve is shifting to the right, which is what it does when the economy is removing itself from a recessionary gap.
6. The price level is higher in Year 2 than in Year 1. The process is illustrated in an exhibit in the relevant chapter of the text. Initially, the AD curve shifts to the right and the economy is in an inflationary gap. To remove itself from an inflationary gap, wage rates rise, and the SRAS curve shifts left (back into long-run equilibrium). Since the economy is back in long-run equilibrium, it is producing Natural Real GDP again. But it is doing this at a higher price level. When the SRAS curve shifts to the left, the price level necessarily rises.

7. The price level is lower in Year 2 than in Year 1. The process is illustrated in an exhibit in the relevant chapter of the text. Initially, the AD curve shifts to the left and the economy is in a recessionary gap. To remove itself from a recessionary gap, wage rates fall, and the SRAS curve shifts right (back into long-run equilibrium). Since the economy is back in long-run equilibrium, it is producing Natural Real GDP again. But it is doing this at a lower price level. When the SRAS curve shifts to the right, the price level necessarily falls.

8. The price level is the same in Year 2 as in Year 1. Initially, the SRAS curve shifts to the left and the price level rises. But then the economy is in a recessionary gap. To remove itself, wage rates fall, and the SRAS curve shifts right (back to its original position). Since the SRAS curve is in its original position, and neither the LRAS curve nor the AD curve have shifted, the price level must be what it was originally (in Year 1).

What Is the Question?

1. These economists believe that Say's law holds in a money economy.

    Who are classical economists?

2. (Current) Real GDP is less than Natural Real GDP.

    What is the condition that specifies a recessionary gap?

3. The economy is operating at Natural Real GDP.

    What is the condition that specifies long-run equilibrium?

4. (Current) Real GDP is greater than Natural Real GDP.

    What is the condition that specifies an inflationary gap?

5. The economy is operating beyond its institutional production possibilities frontier (PPF).

    Where is the economy operating (with respect to its institutional PPF) when it is in an inflationary gap?

6. The economy is operating below its institutional production possibilities frontier (PPF).

    Where is the economy operating (with respect to its institutional PPF) when it is in a recessionary gap.

7. In the long run, the price level is higher, but Real GDP and the unemployment rate are unchanged.

    If the economy is initially in long-run equilibrium, and the economy is self regulating, what will happen to the price level and Real GDP (in the long run) if aggregate demand rises?

8. In the long run, the price level is lower, but Real GDP and the unemployment rate are unchanged.

    If the economy is initially in long-run equilibrium, and the economy is self regulating, what will happen to the price level and Real GDP (in the long run) if aggregate demand falls?

What Is Wrong?

1. The economy is initially in long-run equilibrium. Then, aggregate demand rises. In the short run, the price level and Real GDP rise. If the economy is not self regulating, in the long run the price level has risen and Real GDP has been unchanged (from its initial long-run position).

   The economy is initially in long-run equilibrium. Then, aggregate demand rises. In the short run, the price level and Real GDP rise. If the economy is self regulating, in the long run the price level has risen and Real GDP has been unchanged (from its initial long-run position).

2. The economy is initially in long-run equilibrium. Then, short-run aggregate supply falls. In the short run, the price level and Real GDP rise. If the economy is self regulating, in the long run the price level has fallen back to its original level and Real GDP has been unchanged (from its initial long-run position).

   The economy is initially in long-run equilibrium. Then, short-run aggregate supply falls. In the short run, the price level rises and Real GDP falls. If the economy is self regulating, in the long run the price level has fallen back to its original level and Real GDP has been unchanged (from its initial long-run position).

3. The economy is in a recessionary gap if it is operating at the natural unemployment rate.

   The economy is in long-run equilibrium if it is operating at the natural unemployment rate.

4. The economy is in an inflationary gap if the unemployment rate is greater than the natural unemployment rate.

   The economy is in an inflationary gap if the unemployment rate is less than the natural unemployment rate.

5. The diagram (that follows) shows an economy in a recessionary gap.

   The diagram shows an economy in an inflationary gap.

6. If wage rates fall, the SRAS curve shifts to the left.

   If wage rates fall, the SRAS curve shifts to the right. Alternatively, you could write: If wage rates rise, the SRAS curve shifts to the left.

Multiple Choice
1. c
2. b
3. b
4. c
5. c
6. d
7. a
8. e
9. e
10. d

True-False

    11. F
    12. F
    13. T
    14. F
    15. T

Fill in the Blank

    16. recessionary
    17. rise; leftward
    18. fall; rightward
    19. physical; institutional
    20. Laissez-faire

Chapter 9
Answers

Review Questions

1. Keynes believed that it is possible for consumption to fall, savings to rise, but investment not to rise by the amount that savings has increased. In other words, he did not believe that Say's law necessarily holds in a money economy.
2. Because wage rates are inflexible downward. In other words, wages aren't adjusting in the recessionary gap. If wages don't adjust downward, then the SRAS curve doesn't shift to the right and remove the economy from the recessionary gap.
3. Wages and prices may be inflexible.
4. The price level is constant, there is no foreign sector, and the monetary side of the economy is excluded.
5. $C = Co + MPC (Yd)$, where Co = autonomous consumption, MPC = marginal propensity to consume, and Yd = disposable income.
6. A rise in autonomous consumption, a rise in disposable income, and a rise in the marginal propensity to consume.
7. It is equal to the change in consumption divided by the change in disposable income. $MPC = \Delta C / \Delta Yd$.
8. It is equal to the change in savings divided by the change in disposable income; $\Delta S / \Delta Yd$.
9. Vertically sum consumption, investment, and government purchases at all Real GDP levels. For example, suppose that at Real GDP = Q_1, consumption is $200, investment is $100, and government purchases are $100. It follows that the sum, or $400, is total expenditures. One point on a TE curve represents $400 at Q_1.
10. If inventories rise above the optimum inventory level, firms cut back on production and Real GDP falls. If inventories fall below the optimum inventory level, firms increase production and Real GDP rises. In the process, the economy achieves equilibrium where TP = TE and inventories are at their optimum levels.
11. Inventories fall below their optimum levels, firms increase output, and Real GDP rises. The economy ends up moving from disequilibrium (TE > TP) to equilibrium (TP = TE).
12. Yes, equilibrium is where TE = TP, but there is nothing in the Keynesian framework of analysis that says that where TE = TP, Natural Real GDP has to exist. In other words we can have this condition: TE > TP and Real GDP is either above or below Natural Real GDP.
13. The multiplier = $1 \div (1 - MPC)$. For example, if MPC = 0.80, then the multiplier equals 5.
14. The private sector cannot always remove the economy out of a recessionary gap.

Problems

1.

Change in income	Change in consumption	MPC (marginal propensity to consume)
$2,000	$1,000	0.50
$1,000	$800	0.80
$10,000	$9,500	0.95
$3,456	$2,376	0.6875

2.

If consumption is	And disposable income is	And the marginal propensity to consume is	Then autonomous consumption is
$400	$1,000	0.20	$200
$1,600	$1,900	0.80	$80
$1,700	$2,000	0.75	$200

3.

Consumption	Investment	Net Exports	Total expenditure curve shifts (up, down)
rises	falls by less than consumption rises	rises	up
falls	rises by more than consumption falls	falls by more than investment rises	down
rises	rises	falls by more than investment rises, but falls by less than consumption rises	up

4.

MPC	Multiplier
0.75	4
0.80	5
0.60	2.5

5.

Disposable income	Change in disposable income	Consumption	Change in consumption	Saving
$10,000	$0	$8,200	$0	$1,800
$12,000	$2,000	$9,800	$1,600	$2,200
$14,000	$2,000	$11,400	$1,600	$2,600

6.

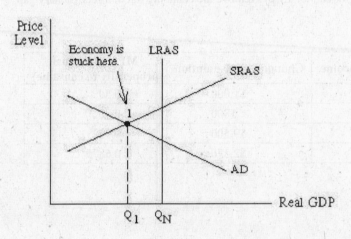

7.

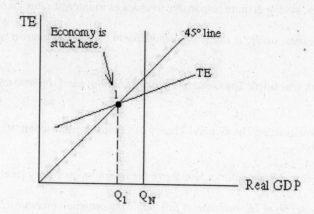

8. At Q_1, TE > TP; at Q_2, TE = TP; at Q_3, TP > TE.

9. Inventories will fall below optimum levels and firms will increase production. Real GDP will begin to rise.

10. Inventories will rise above optimum levels and firms will decrease production. Real GDP will begin to fall.

What Is the Question?

1. Wages and prices may be inflexible.

    What is the Keynesian position on wages and prices?

2. Autonomous consumption.

    What is consumption that is independent of income called?

3. $1 \div (1\text{-MPC})$

    How do you calculate the multiplier?

4. Consumption divided by disposable income.

    What is the average propensity to consume equal to?

5. Inventories rise above optimum levels.

    What initially happens when TP > TE?

What Is Wrong?

1. If the AS curve is horizontal, then an increase in aggregate demand will raise Real GDP, but a decrease in aggregate demand will lower Real GDP and the price level, too.

    A decrease in aggregate demand will not lower the price level if the economy is operating on the horizontal section of the Keynesian AS curve.

2. According to Keynes, saving is more responsive to changes in interest rates than to changes in income.

   According to Keynes, saving is not more responsive to changes in interest rates than to changes in income.

3. Keynes's major work was titled, *The General Theory of Employment, Income and Prices,* and it was published in 1937.

   The major work was titled The General Theory of Employment, Income and Money, *and it was published in 1936.*

4. When TE is greater than TP, inventories rise above the optimum inventory level.

   When TE is greater than TP, inventories fall below the optimum inventory level. Alternatively, you could write: When TP is greater than TE, inventories rise above the optimum inventory level.

5. When the economy is in disequilibrium, inventories are at their optimum levels.

   When the economy is in equilibrium, inventories are at their optimum levels. Alternatively, you could write: When the economy is in disequilibrium, inventories are not at their optimum levels.

Multiple Choice
1. e
2. b
3. c
4. c
5. d
6. b
7. b
8. b
9. b
10. a
11. d
12. b
13. b
14. c
15. b

True-False
16. T
17. T
18. F
19. T
20. T

Fill in the Blank
21. Efficiency wage
22. inflexible
23. AS curve
24. 0.60
25. fall

Chapter 10
Answers

Review Questions

1. If a person earns $40,000 a year, she pays a tax rate of 20 percent. If she earns $45,000 a year, she pays $8,000 plus a tax rate of 25 percent on everything over $40,000 (that is, on the additional $5,000 income).

2. Two people, Smith and Jones, each earn $400 for a job. The $400 is enough to move Smith up into a higher tax (rate) bracket, but not enough to move Jones into a higher tax bracket. At the higher tax bracket (that Smith is now in), the marginal tax rate is 13 percent, but at the lower tax bracket (that Jones is in), the marginal tax rate is 10 percent. It follows, then, that Jones pays a tax rate of 10 percent on the $400 income, but Smith pays a tax rate of 13 percent on the $400 income. Smith's after-tax pay is less than Jones's after-tax pay, although their pay ($400) is exactly the same.

3. The structural deficit is that part of the total budget deficit that would exist even if the economy were operating at full employment. The cyclical deficit is that part of the total budget deficit that is a result of a downturn in the economy.

4. Automatic fiscal policy kicks in automatically when the economy changes. Discretionary fiscal policy is deliberately brought about by Congress. For example, suppose the economy turns down. As a result, unemployment compensation spending rises. Congress doesn't have to meet to direct increases in unemployment compensation spending; it is simply the result of more people (during economic bad times) losing their jobs and collecting unemployment compensation. This is an example of automatic fiscal policy. If the Congress meets, proposes legislation to cut income tax rates, and then passes the legislation (all in order to jump start the economy), then this is an example of discretionary fiscal policy.

5. Expansionary fiscal policy (lower taxes, increases in government expenditures). Expansionary fiscal policy will raise aggregate demand (if there is either zero or incomplete crowding out) and thus reduce or eliminate the recessionary gap.

6. For every $1 increase in government spending, private spending falls by $0.60.

7. No, more government spending on libraries does not necessarily lead to less private spending on books. If it does, though, there is some degree of crowding out. Our point is that there doesn't have to be crowding out.

8. If the budget is initially balanced, and then spending rises, a budget deficit occurs. Government will need to borrow to finance the deficit. As a result, the demand for credit (or loanable funds) rises, and the interest rate rises. If the U.S. interest rate is now higher than foreign interest rates, foreigners will want to buy U.S. interest-paying Treasury securities. To do this, they need to supply their home currency and demand U.S. dollars. The increased demand for U.S. dollars will lead to an appreciation in the value of the dollar.

9. No, it is not necessarily the case that interest rates rise. Because of the deficit, the demand for credit (or loanable funds) will rise. But the supply of loanable funds may rise, too. This will happen if individuals translate a higher budget today into higher taxes in the future. They will end up saving more today in order to pay the higher taxes in the future. The increased saving will put downward pressure on interest rates. Will interest rates rise, fall, or remain constant on net? It depends on the increase in the demand for loanable funds relative to the increase in the supply of loanable funds.

10. It is the time after policymakers decide on what type of fiscal policy measure is required and the actual passage of the fiscal policy measure.

11. Suppose the economy's SRAS curve is shifting to the right, but this is unknown to policymakers. They institute expansionary fiscal policy and push the AD curve rightward more than they would have had they known the SRAS curve is shifting right. In the end, the economy goes from a recessionary gap to an inflationary gap. This process is described in an exhibit in the relevant chapter of the text.

12. Suppose someone earns and income of $40,000 and pays $10,000 in income taxes. His average tax rate is equal to his income taxes divided by his income, or 25 percent. Now suppose the person earns an additional $1,000, and must pay $333 additional income taxes as a result. His marginal tax rate is the change in his taxes ($333) divided by the change in his income ($1,000), or 33 percent.

13. Not necessarily. Higher income tax rates will raise tax revenue if the economy is on the upward-sloping portion of the Laffer curve; higher income tax rates will lower tax revenue if the economy is on the downward-sloping portion of the Laffer curve.

Problems
1. $1,500
2. $2,372
3. $3,558.32
4. 12 percent
5. 14 percent; 10.756 percent
6.

Total budget deficit	Structural deficit	Cyclical deficit
$250 billion	$100 billion	$150 billion
$100 billion	$25 billion	$75 billion
$150 billion	$100 billion	$50 billion

7. Yes, if expansionary fiscal policy can shift the AD curve to the right by enough to intersect the LRAS curve at point 2.

8. The economy is initially at point 1 in a recessionary gap. Unbeknownst to policymakers, the SRAS curve is shifting to the right. Policymakers enact expansionary fiscal policy and shift the aggregate demand curve from AD_1 to AD_2. They hope to move the economy to point 1A. Instead, since the SRAS curve has shifted to the right from $SRAS_1$ to $SRAS_2$, the economy moves from point 1 to 2, from a recessionary gap into an inflationary gap.

9.

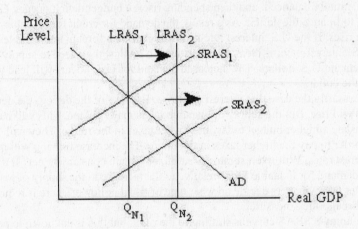

10.

Income	Taxes Paid	Marginal tax rate	Average tax rate
$10,000	$2,200	22 percent	22 percent
$11,000	$2,900	70 percent	26.36 percent
$12,000	$3,700	80 percent	30.83 percent

11.

Taxable income	Tax rate	Tax revenue
$100 million	12.3 percent	$12.3 million
$190 million	10.0 percent	$19 million
$200 million	9.0 percent	$18 million

What Is the Question?

1. The same tax rate is used for all income levels.

    What is a proportional income tax?

2. A different tax rate is used for different income levels.

    What is a progressive or regressive tax rate structure?

3. It is equal to the total budget deficit minus the cyclical deficit.

    What is the structural budget deficit equal to?

4. Changes in government expenditures and/or taxes that occur automatically without (additional) congressional action.

    What is automatic fiscal policy?

5. Saving increases as a result of the higher future taxes implied by the deficit.

    What do new classical economists think will happen to saving if the budget deficit rises?

6. The time if takes before policymakers know of a change in the economy.

    What is the data lag?

7. The change in the tax payment divided by the change in taxable income.

    What is the marginal tax rate?

8. The downward-sloping part of the Laffer curve.

    Higher tax rates bring about lower tax revenues in what part of the Laffer curve? Alternatively, you could write, Lower tax rates bring about higher tax revenues in what part of the Laffer curve?

Multiple Choice

1. e
2. d
3. d
4. c
5. e
6. b
7. b
8. b
9. b
10. e
11. c
12. a
13. b
14. c
15. b

True-False

16. T
17. T
18. T
19. F
20. T

Fill in the Blank

21. 106
22. marginal
23. downward-sloping
24. tax rate
25. Crowding out

Chapter 11
Answers

Review Questions

1. Here is an example in a barter economy: Bob has a Swiss army knife and wants a telephone. Jack has a telephone and wants a Swiss army knife. Here is an example in a money economy: Harry has $40 and wants a shirt. Mike has a shirt and wants $40.
2. It means money serves as a common measurement in which relative values are expressed. Stated differently, it means money serves as the "common language" in which relative values are expressed.
3. It is out of self interest that people (in a barter economy) try to reduce the costs of making exchanges. They simply want to make their lives easier. In pursuit of this goal, they begin to accept the good that is the most marketable of all goods. In time, this good emerges into money. The people didn't intend for there to be money; they intended only to make their lives easier.
4. With money, people do not have to take as much time finding the person with whom they have a double coincidence of wants. Everyone will take money. With less time spent making exchanges, people have more time to work and/or play.
5. Money is valuable because it is generally accepted by everyone.
6. Currency held outside banks plus checkable deposits plus traveler's checks
7. M_1 plus savings deposits (including money market deposit accounts) plus small-denomination time deposits plus money market mutual funds.
8. A money is not only widely accepted for purposes of exchange, but also in the repayment of debt. A credit card debt cannot be paid off with your credit card. A credit card is not money, it is a loan.
9. A bank's reserves consist of vault cash and bank deposits at the Fed.
10. Certainly if checkable deposits rise, required reserves will rise, too. Required reserves = r x Checkable deposits. Whether or not the bank will have to hold more reserves depends on what reserves it is currently holding. For example, suppose checkable deposits = $400 million and the required-reserve ratio is 10 percent. It follows that required reserves are $40 million. Now, suppose the bank is holding $50 million in reserves. It is holding more reserves than it has to. What happens if checkable deposits now rise to $500 million. Required reserves are now $50 million. Will the bank have to hold more reserves than it is presently holding? Not at all. It is holding the amount of reserves ($50 million) that it is supposed to be holding. Of course, if was only holding $40 million in reserves before, it would have to hold $10 million more in reserves.
11. George sells a television set and receives a $400 check for it. He takes the check to his bank, asks for $100 cash, and deposits the remainder, $300, into his checking account. The $100 is a cash leakage.
12. The simple deposit multiplier is 1 divided by the required-reserve ratio (1/r). The required-reserve ratio is the percentage of each dollar that is deposited in a bank that must be held in reserve form.

Problems

1.

Required-reserve ratio	Simple deposit multiplier
0.10	10
0.12	8.33
0.09	11.11

2.

Currency	Checkable deposits	Traveler's checks	M₁ money supply
$200 billion	$500 billion	$8 billion	$708 billion
$100 billion	$591 billion	$9 billion	$700 billion
$190 billion	$300 billion	$10 billion	$500 billion

3.

Checkable deposits	Required-reserve ratio	Required reserves
$400 million	0.10	$40 million
$300 million	0.12	$36 million
$1,000 million	0.15	$150 million

4.

Checkable deposits	Required-reserve ratio	Required reserves	Reserves	Excess reserves
$400 million	0.10	$40 million	$60 million	$20 million
$500 million	0.15	$75 million	$80 million	$5 million
$872 million	0.12	$104.64 million	$200 million	$95.36 million

5.

Checkable deposits	Required-reserve ratio	Required reserves	Vault cash	Bank deposits at the Fed	Excess reserves
$230 million	0.13	$29.9 million	$10 million	$30 million	$10.1 million
$367 million	0.10	$36.7 million	$1 million	$43 million	$ 7.3 million
$657 million	0.12	$78.84 million	$23 million	$60 million	$4.16 million

6.

Change in reserves	Required-reserve ratio	Maximum change in the money supply
+ $4 million	0.10	$40 million
+ $50 million	0.12	$416.67 million
– $41 million	0.10	– $410 million

7.

Checkable deposits	Required-reserve ratio	Required reserves	Vault cash	Bank deposits at the Fed	Excess reserves
$1,000 million	0.10	$100 million	$50 million	$50 million	$0
$230 million	0.12	$27.6 million	$20 million	$7.6 million	$0
$498 million	0.10	$49.8 million	$10 million	$39.8 million	$0

What Is the Question?

1. Medium of exchange, unit of account, and store of value.

    What are the three functions of money?

2. Exchanging goods and services for other goods and services.

    What is barter?

3. The least exclusive function of money.

    What is the store-of-value function of money?

4. General acceptability.

    What gives money its value?

5. Deposits on which checks can be written.

    What are demand deposits?

6. An asset that can easily and quickly be turned into cash.

    What is a liquid asset?

7. The central bank of the United States.

    What is the Fed (or the Federal Reserve System)?

8. Bank deposits at the Fed plus vault cash.

    What are reserves equal to?

9. The difference between reserves and required reserves.

    What are excess reserves equal to?

10. 1 divided by the required-reserve ratio.

    What is the simple deposit multiplier equal to?

What Is Wrong?

1. How much money did you earn last week?

    How much income did you earn last week?

2. A double coincidence of wants is not a necessary condition for trade to take place.

    A double coincidence of wants is a necessary condition for trade to take place.

3. The largest component of M_1 is currency.

    The largest component of M_1 is checkable deposits.

4. M_1 is the broad definition of the money supply.

    M_1 is the narrow definition of the money supply. Alternatively, you could write: M_2 is the broad definition of the money supply.

5. Excess reserves equal reserves plus required reserves.

    Excess reserves equal reserves minus required reserves.

6. The maximum change in checkable deposits = r x ΔR.

    The maximum change in checkable deposits = 1/r x ΔR

7. The greater the cash leakages, the larger the increase in the money supply for a given positive change in reserves.

    The greater the cash leakages, the smaller the increase in the money supply for a given positive change in reserves. Alternatively, you could write: The smaller the cash leakages, the larger the increase in the money supply for a given positive change in reserves.

8. Our money today has value because it is backed by gold.

    Our money today has value because of its general acceptability. Alternatively, you could write, Our money today is not backed by gold.

Multiple Choice
1. e
2. c
3. c
4. b
5. b
6. d
7. a
8. d
9. b
10. a
11. a
12. c
13. a
14. c
15. d

True-False
16. T
17. F
18. T
19. T
20. F

Fill in the Blank
21. double coincidence of wants
22. Reserves
23. fractional reserve
24. 10
25. general acceptability

Chapter 12
Answers

Review Questions
1. Seven
2. Twelve
3. Boston, New York, Philadelphia, Cleveland, Richmond, Atlanta, Dallas, Chicago, St. Louis, Minneapolis, Kansas City, San Francisco
4. control the money supply
5. There are 12 members of the FOMC. Seven of the 12 are the Board of Governors of the Federal Reserve System, one is the president of the New York Fed, and the remaining four are (on a rotating basis) presidents of the remaining 11 Fed banks.
6. A person endorses a check and turns it over to her bank. The bank sends it to its Federal Reserve District bank. If the check was written on a bank in another Fed district, then the Fed bank sends the check to the Fed bank in that district. The Fed bank in that district sends the check to the bank on which the check was written. What about funds? Funds are moved from the reserve account of the bank on which the check is written into the reserve account of the bank in which the recipient of the check has an account.
7. The Treasury is a budgetary agency; its job is to collect taxes and borrow funds to manage the affairs of the federal government. The Fed is a monetary agency. Its major responsibility is to control the money supply.
8. The Fed buys $10 million of government securities from, say, Bank A. It pays for the purchase by increasing the balance of Bank A's reserve account by $10 million. Thus, Bank A has $10 million more in reserves. As a result of increased reserves, Bank A ends up with more excess reserves, which it uses to create loans. As it extends loans to customers, it creates checkable deposits which are part of the money supply. The money supply rises.
9. The Fed lowers the discount rate and banks begin to borrow from the Fed. The Fed extends loans to these banks by increasing the balance in their reserve accounts. The banks end up with more excess reserves which they use to create loans. As the banks extend loans, they create checkable deposits which are part of the money supply. The money supply rises.
10. Suppose checkable deposits = $400 million, the required-reserve ratio is 10 percent, required reserves are $40 million, reserves are $40 million, and excess reserves are $0. Now suppose the required-reserve ratio is lowered to 5 percent. Required reserves now fall from $40 million to $20 million. This means reserves minus required reserves (or excess reserves) are now $20 million instead of $0. Banks use the excess reserves to create new loans and checkable deposits and so the money supply rises.
11. The discount rate is set by the Fed (specifically, the Board of Governors of the Fed). There are no market forces that determine the discount rate. The federal funds rate is set by the supply of, and demand for, reserves. The federal funds rate is set in a market, the discount rate is not.

Problems
1. Checkable deposits = $400 million
    Required-reserve ratio = 5 percent
    Required reserves = $20 million
    Reserves = $40 million
    Excess reserves = $20 million

2. Checkable deposits = $500 million
    Required-reserve ratio = 12 percent
    Required reserves = $60 million
    Reserves = $70 million
    Excess reserves = $10 million

3.   Checkable deposits = $610 million
        Required-reserve ratio = 10 percent
        Required reserves = $61 million
        Reserves = $70 million
        Excess reserves = $9 million

4.   Checkable deposits = $600 million
        Required-reserve ratio = 10 percent
        Required reserves = $60 million
        Reserves = $70 million
        Excess reserves = $10 million

5.

Fed action…	Money supply (rises, falls, remains unchanged)
Conducts an open market purchase	rises
Lowers required-reserve ratio	rises
Raises the discount rate to a level higher than the federal funds rate	falls
Conducts an open market sale	falls
Lowers the discount rate to a level substantially lower than the federal funds rate	rises
Raises the required-reserve ratio	falls

6.

Fed action…	Maximum change in the money supply
Buys $100 million worth of government securities from Bank A	$1,000 million
Gives a $10 million discount loan to Bank B	$100 million
Sells $20 million worth of government securities to Bank C	– $200 million

What Is the Question?

1.   Any of these changes in Fed policy tools will cause the money supply to rise.

     What will a decrease in the required-reserve ratio, an open market purchase, and a decrease in the discount rate (relative to the federal funds rate) do to the money supply?

2.   This group conducts open market operations.

     What is the Federal Open Market Committee (FOMC)?

3.   These are sold to raise funds to pay the government's bills.

     What are U.S. Treasury securities?

4.   The Fed buys and sells government securities.

     What is an open market operation?

5.   Either to the federal funds market or to the Fed for a discount loan.

   Where can a bank go to obtain a loan?

What Is Wrong?

1.   The president of the St. Louis Fed holds a permanent seat on the FOMC.

   The president of the New York Fed holds a permanent seat on the FOMC.

2.   The Fed is a budgetary and monetary agency and the Treasury is a budgetary agency only.

   The Fed is a monetary agency and the Treasury is a budgetary agency.

3.   An open market purchase refers to a commercial bank buying government securities from the Fed.

   An open market purchase refers to the Fed buying government securities from a commercial bank. Alternatively, you could write: An open market sale refers to a commercial bank buying government securities from the Fed. (The Fed sells.)

4.   An increase in the discount rate is likely to raise the money supply.

   A decrease in the discount rate is likely to raise the money supply. Alternatively, you could write: An increase in the discount rate is likely to lower the money supply.

5.   The major responsibility of the Fed is to clear checks.

   The major responsibility of the Fed is to control the money supply.

Multiple Choice
   1.   a
   2.   b
   3.   a
   4.   d
   5.   c
   6.   d
   7.   b
   8.   e
   9.   d
   10. b

True-False
   11. T
   12. T
   13. T
   14. F
   15. F

Fill in the Blank
   16. rise; decline
   17. federal funds rate
   18. New York
   19. open market purchase
   20. remain unchanged

Chapter 13
Answers

Review Questions

1. If $1 changes hands 3 times (in a year) to buy goods and services, then velocity is 3.
2. The equation of exchange is simply an identify. It simply says that the money supply multiplied by velocity equals the price level multiplied by Real GDP. Stated differently, it says that total spending must equal total receipts. The simply quantity theory of money is a theory that offers a particular prediction. The simple quantity theory of money is built on the equation of exchange. It assumes that two of the variables in the equation (velocity and Real GDP) are constant; then it predicts that changes in the money supply lead to strictly proportional changes in the price level.
3. The simple quantity theory of money predicts that changes in the money supply lead to strictly proportional changes in the price level.
4. In the simple quantity theory of money, Real GDP is constant. It follows, then, that the AS curve is vertical.
5. The equation of exchange is MV = PQ. What will cause an increase in P (inflation)? The answer is an increase in M and V and a decrease in Q. What will cause a decrease in P (deflation)? The answer is a decrease in M and V and an increase in Q.
6. a. The SRAS curve is upward sloping.
   b. the money supply and velocity
   c. Velocity changes in a predictable way.
   d. The economy is self regulating, prices and wages are flexible.
7. Yes, we agree. Either a rightward shift in the AD curve, or a leftward shift in the SRAS curve, can cause the price level to rise.
8. It is a demand-side phenomenon. It is caused by continued increases in aggregate demand.
9. The liquidity effect refers to the change in the interest rate that is brought about by a change in the supply of loanable funds.
10. The expectations effect refers to the change in the interest rate that is brought about by a change in the expected inflation rate.
11. A change in the money supply can affect the interest rate via the liquidity, income, price-level, and expectations effects.
12. The nominal interest rate is equal to the real interest rate plus the expected inflation rate. The real interest rate is the nominal interest rate minus the expected inflation rate.

Problems

1.

Percentage change in the money supply	Percentage change in the price level
+25	+25
− 10	− 10
+9	+9

2.

Money supply	Velocity	Real GDP	Will there be inflation or deflation?
rises	rises	stays constant	inflation
falls	stays constant	rises	deflation
falls	falls	rises	deflation

3. In the short run the price level and Real GDP will rise. In the long run, only the price level will rise.
4. In the short run the price level and Real GDP will fall. In the long run, only the price level will fall.
5.

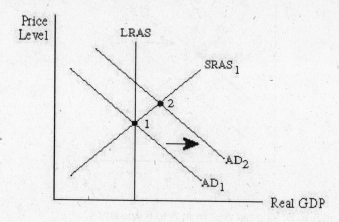

6.

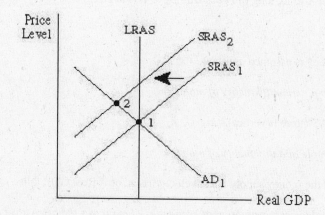

7. The SRAS curve would continually shift to the left, and while the price level would continually rise, Real GDP (Q) would get increasingly smaller.

8.

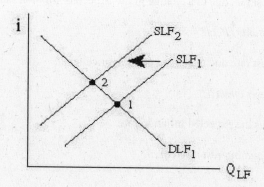

9.

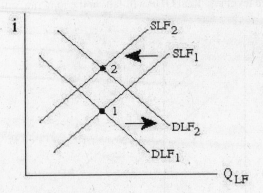

10. short run goes from A to B; long run goes from A to F (via B)
11. short run goes from A to D; long run goes from A to E (via D)

What Is the Question?

1. In the theory, velocity is assumed constant.

    What is the simple quantity theory of money?

2. In the theory, the AS curve is vertical.

    What is the simple quantity theory of money?

3. This can happen if the money supply rises, velocity rises, or if Real GDP falls.

    Using the variables in the equation of exchange, what causes the price level to rise?

4. According to these economists, changes in velocity can change aggregate demand.

    Who are the monetarists?

5. The change in the interest rate due to a change in the expected inflation rate.

    What is the expectations effect?

6. The change in the interest rate due to a change in the price level.

    What is the price-level effect?

7. The real interest rate plus the expected inflation rate.

    What does the nominal interest rate equal?

What Is Wrong?

1. An increase in velocity and a decrease in Real GDP will lead to a decline in the price level.

    An increase in the velocity and a decrease in Real GDP will lead to an increase *in the price level.*

2. In both the simple quantity theory of money and the monetarist theory, the aggregate demand curve will shift right or left if either the money supply or interest rates change.

    In the simple quantity theory of money, the AD curve will shift right or left if the money supply changes. In monetarist theory, the AD curve will shift right or left if either the money supply or velocity change.

3. According to monetarists, prices are flexible but wages are inflexible.

    According to monetarists, both prices and wages are flexible.

4. The CPI rises from 100 to 120, to 130, to 135, to 145, and so on. This is indicative of one-shot inflation.

    This is indicative of continued inflation.

5. Continued decreases in short-run aggregate supply can lead to continued deflation.

    Continued decreases in short-run aggregate supply can lead to continued inflation.

Multiple Choice
1. e
2. b
3. d
4. e
5. e
6. c
7. e
8. c
9. b
10. b
11. d
12. d
13. b
14. e

True-False
15. F
16. F
17. F
18. F
19. T

Fill in the Blank
20. demand-induced
21. supply-induced
22. money supply
23. demand for; supply of
24. real interest rate

Chapter 14
Answers

Review Questions

1. People will hold more money the lower the opportunity cost of holding money. The opportunity cost of holding money is the interest rate. As the interest rate falls (the opportunity cost of holding money falls) and people will hold more money, *ceteris paribus*.

2. If investment is not interest insensitive, and there is no liquidity trap, then the Keynesian transmission mechanism will work for an increase in the money supply as follows: An increase in the money supply lowers the interest rate; as the interest rate falls, investment rises; greater investment leads to higher aggregate demand. Higher aggregate demand leads to greater Real GDP.

3. If there is a surplus of money, the interest rate falls; if there is a shortage of money, the interest rate rises.

4. If investment is interest insensitive it means that changes in the interest rate do not lead to changes in investment. If investment is interest insensitive, then the Keynesian transmission mechanism is short-circuited; the link to the money market and goods and services market is broken. It follows that changes in the money market will not affect the goods and services market. Monetary policy is ineffective at changing Real GDP.

5. If Bond A pays 10 percent interest each year, and a new bond (Bond B) is offered that pays 12 percent interest each year, then no one will buy Bond A at the same price they would pay for Bond B. The price of Bond A will have to fall to make it competitive with Bond B. In short, the prices of existing bonds (like Bond A) move down as current interest rates rise.

6. The monetarist transmission mechanism is direct: changes in the money market directly impact the goods and services market. For example, a rise in the money supply will create a surplus of money at the given interest rate. This surplus of money will go to buy goods and services.

7. Expansionary monetary policy refers to an increase in the money supply. Contractionary monetary policy refers to a decrease in the money supply.

8. Expansionary monetary policy (increase in the money supply) is supposed to increase aggregate demand. As the AD curve shifts to the right, the economy begins to produce more Real GDP and thus the recessionary gap is eliminated.

9. Contractionary monetary policy (decrease in the money supply) is supposed to decrease aggregate demand. As the AD curve shifts to the left, the economy begins to produce less Real GDP at a lower price level and thus the inflationary gap is eliminated.

10. a) the economy does not always equilibrate quickly enough at Natural Real GDP; b) activist monetary policy is effective at smoothing out the business cycle; c) activist monetary policy is flexible.

11. Expansionary monetary policy is supposed to remove the economy from Point 1 to Point 2. However, if the SRAS curve is shifting to the right, and monetary authorities do not take this into account, then the economy will move from Point 1 (recessionary gap) to an inflationary gap (Point 3).

Problems

1.

If the money supply...	And the demand for money curve is...	And investment is...	Then Real GDP will (rise, fall, remain unchanged)
rises	downward sloping	interest sensitive	rise
falls	horizontal	interest sensitive	remain unchanged
rises	downward sloping	interest insensitive	remain unchanged
falls	downward sloping	interest sensitive	fall
rises	horizontal	interest sensitive	remain unchanged

2.

If the money supply…	And the demand for money curve is…	And investment is…	Then Real GDP will (rise, fall, remain unchanged)
rises	downward sloping	interest sensitive	rises
falls	downward sloping	interest sensitive	falls
rises	downward sloping	interest insensitive	rises
falls	downward sloping	interest insensitive	falls

3.

If the money supply…	And the demand for money curve is…	And investment is…	Then the price level will (rise, fall, remain unchanged)
rises	downward sloping	interest sensitive	remain unchanged
falls	horizontal	interest sensitive	remain unchanged
rises	downward sloping	interest insensitive	remain unchanged
falls	downward sloping	interest sensitive	remain unchanged
rises	horizontal	interest sensitive	remain unchanged

4. A surplus of money will cause the AD curve to shift to the right.

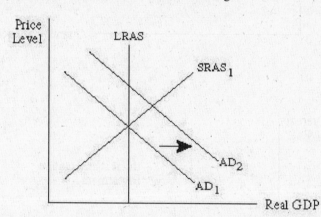

5. A surplus of money will cause the interest rate to fall, which will cause investment to rise, which will cause the AD curve to shift to the right.

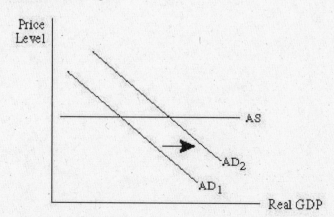

6. It will end up higher because the AD curve has shifted to the right.
7. It will end up lower because the AD curve has shifted to the left.
8.

Percentage change in velocity	Percentage change in Real GDP	Percentage change in the money supply
+ 2 percent	+ 3 percent	+ 1 percent
− 1 percent	+ 2 percent	+ 3 percent
+ 2 percent	− 3 percent	− 5 percent

9.

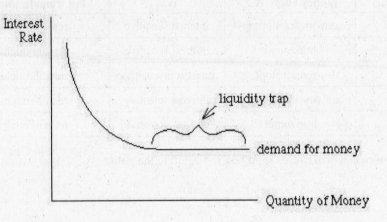

10.

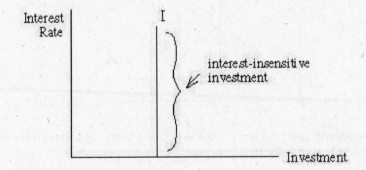

11.

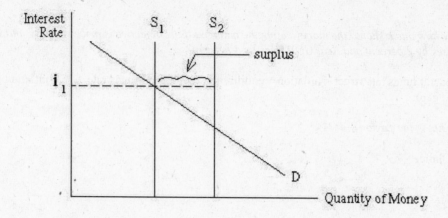

12.

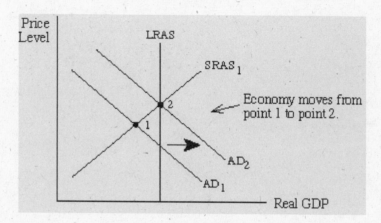

What Is the Question?

1.   The money supply rises but the interest rate does not fall.

     What happens when the money supply rises but the economy is in a liquidity trap?

2.   The interest rate falls, but investment does not increase.

     What happens if investment is insensitive and the interest rate falls?

3.   A change in the money supply directly leads to a change in aggregate demand.

     How does the monetarist transmission mechanism work if there is a change in the money supply?

4.   Activist monetary policy may not work, activist monetary policy may be destabilizing, and wages and prices are sufficiently flexible to allow the economy to equilibrate at reasonable speed at Natural Real GDP.

     What are the arguments against activist monetary policy?

5. If velocity rises by 2 percent, and Real GDP rises by 3 percent, then increase the money supply by 1 percent.

    By how much should the money supply be changed if the objective is price stability and velocity rises by 2 percent and Real GDP rises by 3 percent?

6. The federal funds rate target = inflation + equilibrium real federal funds rate + 1/2 (inflation gap) + 1/2 (output gap).

    What is the Taylor Rule?

Multiple Choice
1. d
2. a
3. c
4. b
5. d
6. b
7. c
8. d
9. a
10. d
11. a
12. b
13. c
14. d

True-False
15. T
16. F
17. F
18. F
19. F

Fill in the Blank
20. insensitive; liquidity trap
21. directly
22. contractionary; expansionary
23. equilibrium real federal funds rate
24. Inflation targeting

Chapter 15
Answers

Review Questions

1. A. W. Phillips identified the relationship between wage inflation and unemployment. Samuelson and Solow identified the relationship between price inflation and unemployment.
2. If the Phillips curve is downward sloping, then there is a tradeoff between inflation and unemployment. High inflation goes with low unemployment and low inflation goes with high unemployment. Stagflation—which is both high inflation and high unemployment—cannot occur.
3. According to Friedman, when there is a difference between the expected and actual inflation rates, there is a tradeoff between inflation and unemployment. In short, workers can be "fooled" into believing their real wages are higher than in fact they are. In time, workers learn, and the expected inflation rate equals the actual inflation rate. When this occurs, there is no tradeoff between inflation and unemployment.
4. Consider the issue of inflation. What will the inflation rate be over the next year? With adaptive expectations, a person only considers what the inflation rate has been in forming his expected inflation rate. With rational expectations, a person considers what the inflation rate has been, what is happening now in the economy, and what he thinks will happen in the future in the economy when forming his expected inflation rate.
5. Because workers are sometimes "fooled" into thinking their real wages are higher than they are.
6. No. If policy is unanticipated, we get the same results whether individuals hold adaptive or rational expectations.
7. Yes. With adaptive expectations, there is a change in Real GDP in the short run; with rational expectations, there is no change in Real GDP.
8. Changes in Real GDP can originate on the supply-side of the economy. In other words, changes in LRAS can bring about changes in Real GDP (ups and downs in Real GDP). Moreover, most business cycle theorists not only believe that changes in Real GDP can originate on the supply-side of the economy, but do originate on the supply-side of the economy.
9. The PIP says that under certain conditions (such as flexible wages and prices, rational expectations, and correctly anticipated policy) expansionary fiscal and monetary policy is ineffective at meeting macroeconomic objectives (such as increasing Real GDP or lowering the unemployment rate).
10. Expectations are formed rationally and some prices and wages are inflexible.
11. Yes. Changes in AD or LRAS can change Real GDP.

Problems
1.

Starting point	People hold	Change in the economy	Change is	Prices and wages are	Short run change in Real GDP (rise, fall, remain unchanged)	Long run change in the price level (rise, fall, remain unchanged)
Long-run equilibrium	adaptive expectations	AD rises	unanticipated	flexible	rise	rise
Long-run equilibrium	rational expectations	AD rises	correctly anticipated	flexible	remain unchanged	rise
Long-run equilibrium	rational expectations	AD rises	unanticipated	flexible	rise	rise

259

2.   The economy will move from Point 1 to Point 2.

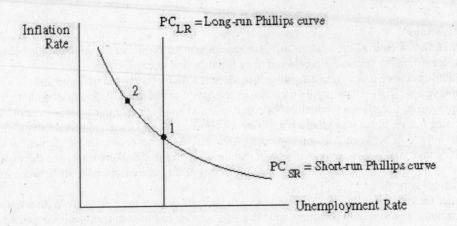

3.   The economy will move from Point 1 to Point 2 on the long-run Phillips curve.

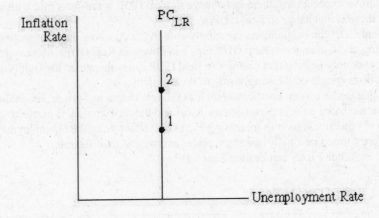

4.   The economy will move from Point 1 to Point 2 if some wages and prices are inflexible. It will move from Point 1 to Point 3 if wages and prices are flexible.

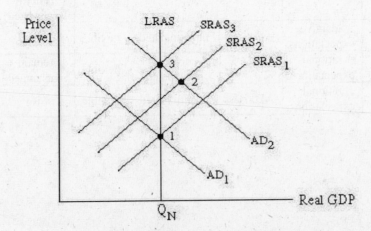

5. Real GDP might be lower because the money supply has fallen and therefore the AD curve has shifted to the left. But it need not be. It could be lower because the LRAS curve first shifted to the left, lowering Real GDP, and later the money supply fell. In other words, the real cause of the lower Real GDP was a decline in LRAS, not a decline in the money supply (originating on the demand-side of the economy).

6. The economy moves from Point 1 to Point 2.

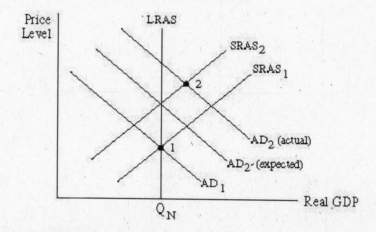

7. The economy moves from Point 1 to Point 2.

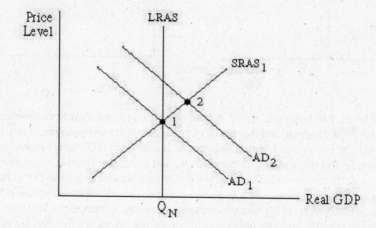

8.   The economy moves from Point 1 to Point 2.

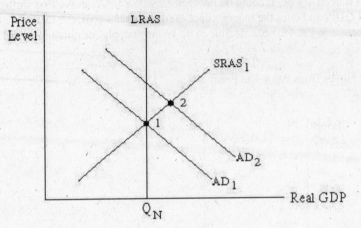

9.

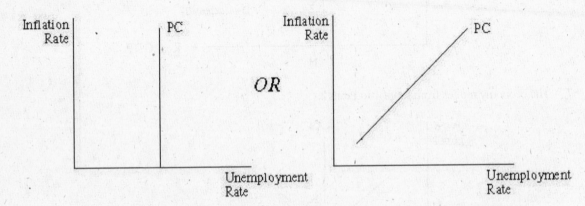

10. It says the PIP holds. PIP holds that policy cannot bring about certain macroeconomic outcomes. If
     there is only one Phillips curve, and it is always vertical, then the unemployment rate is not changing.
     This is likely to be at the natural unemployment rate. Increases in AD, then, cannot change the
     unemployment rate. But this can only occur if wages and prices are flexible, expectations are rational,
     and policy is correctly anticipated. These are the conditions necessary for the PIP to hold.
11. If there is only one Phillips curve, and it is always vertical, then the unemployment rate is not
     changing. This is likely to be at the natural unemployment rate. Increases in AD, then, cannot change
     the unemployment rate. But this can only occur if wages and prices are flexible, expectations are
     rational, and policy is correctly anticipated.

What Is the Question?

1.   It posited an inverse relationship between wage inflation and unemployment.

     *What type of relationship did the original Phillips curve (by A.W. Phillips) posit between wage
     inflation and unemployment?*

2.   In the short run, the economy moves away from its natural unemployment rate, but in the long run, the
     economy operates at its natural unemployment rate.

     *What happens in the short run and long run in the Friedman natural rate theory as a result of an
     increase in aggregate demand?*

3. The expected inflation rate changes faster in this theory.

    What is rational expectations theory (as opposed to adaptive expectations theory)?

4. Expectations are rational and some prices and wages are inflexible.

    What are two assumptions of New Keynesian theory?

5. Stagflation is precluded.

    What does a downward-sloping Phillips curve preclude?

6. According to this theory, there is a tradeoff between inflation and unemployment—but only in the short run.

    What does the Friedman natural rate theory say about the tradeoff between inflation and unemployment in the short run and in the long run?

7. Initially, both Real GDP and the price level fall. Later, the money supply may decline.

    What does business cycle theory say about the sequencing of changes in Real GDP, the price level, and the money supply?

What Is Wrong?

1. Stagflation over time is consistent with a short-run Phillips curve that continually shifts to the left.

    Stagflation over time is consistent with a short-run Phillips curve that continually shifts to the right. Alternatively, you could write: Stagflation over time is not consistent with a short-run Phillips curve that continually shifts to the left.

2. If the economy is in long-run equilibrium, then it is not on the long-run vertical Phillips curve.

    If the economy is in long-run equilibrium, then it is on the long-run Phillips curve.

3. Rational expectations theory assumes that people are smarter today than they were yesterday, but not as smart as they will be tomorrow.

    Rational expectations theory assumes that people base their expected inflation rate on past inflation rates, and on the policy effects of what is currently occurring (in the present) and what may happen (in the future).

4. In real business cycle theory, the LRAS curve shifts to the left after the money supply has fallen.

    In real business cycle theory, the LRAS curve shifts to the left before the money supply falls.

5. New Keynesian theory holds that wages are not completely flexible because of things such as rational expectations.

    New Keynesians hold that wages are not completely flexible because of things such as long-term contracts.

6.   The policy ineffectiveness proposition holds under the conditions that (1) policy changes are anticipated correctly, (2) wages and prices are flexible, and (3) expectations are adaptive.

The policy ineffectiveness proposition holds under the conditions that (1) policy changes are anticipated correctly, (2) wages and prices are flexible, and (3) expectations are rational.

Multiple Choice
1.   d
2.   b
3.   b
4.   a
5.   b
6.   b
7.   c
8.   e
9.   d
10. a
11. d
12. a
13. c
14. a
15. d

True-False
16. F
17. F
18. T
19. F
20. T

Fill in the Blank
21. long-run equilibrium
22. Stagflation
23. New classical
24. supply-side
25. new classical theory

Chapter 16
Answers

Review Questions

1. Absolute real economic growth is an increase in Real GDP from one period to the next. Per capita real economic growth is an increase in per capita Real GDP (Real GDP divided by population) from one period to the next.
2. It means it occurs from a point below the production possibilities frontier (PPF). If the economy is at a point below its PPF, there are some unemployed resources.
3. It means it occurs from a point on the PPF. With economic growth from an efficient level of production, the PPF shifts rightward.
4. It means a country does not need natural resources to experience economic growth, and if a country does have natural resources it is not guaranteed that it will experience economic growth.
5. Human capital is education, training, and experience.
6. Combining people (labor) with certain capital goods makes people more productive. A person with a tractor is more productive at farming than a person with a stick. Capital investment refers to purchases of capital goods. As capital investment rises, the people that work with the capital become more productive.
7. The critics argue that it is difficult, if not impossible, for government officials to figure out which industries are most likely to be successful in the global marketplace. They also argue that government is likely to respond and turn industrial policy into some form of political policy, where certain industries are assisted, not based on their merit, but on their political power.
8. labor and capital
9. It means that technology is part of the economic system as opposed to being outside the economic system. Since technology is endogenous, it follows that people can do certain things to promote it.
10. Ideas, specifically ideas on how to rearrange resources in valuable ways, are what cause economic growth.
11. It means that when we take what is given—the resources that exist—and rearrange them in different ways, we sometimes come up with a more valuable arrangement than existed before. This new, more valuable arrangement is critical to the process of economic growth.
12. Yes. Suppose economic growth occurs as a result of the LRAS curve shifting to the right. If AD does not change, then the price level will fall.

Problems

1.

If the annual growth rate in Real GDP is	then it will take _____ years for the economy to double in size.
3 percent	24
4 percent	18
5 percent	14.4

2. A movement from Point 1 to Point 2.

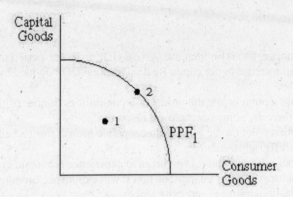

3. A movement from Point 1 on PPF₁ to Point 2 on PPF₂.

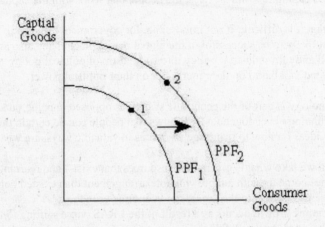

4. A movement from Point 1 to Point 2.

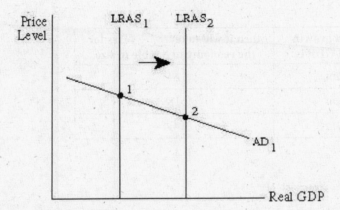

5. A movement from Point 1 to Point 2.

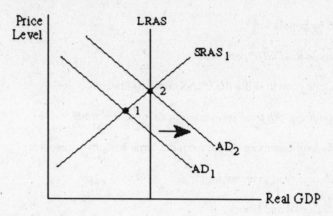

6. A movement from Point 1 to Point 2.

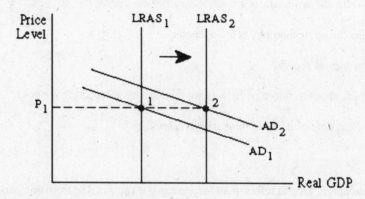

7. A movement from Point 1 to Point 2.

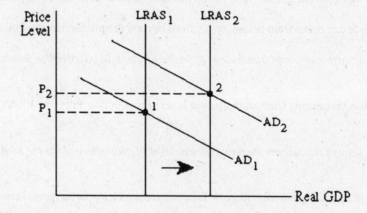

What Is the Question?

1. Real GDP divided by population.

    How is per capita Real GDP computed?

2. This type of economic growth shifts the LRAS curve rightward.

    What is economic growth from an efficient level of production?

3. It makes it possible to obtain more output from the same amount of resources.

    What is an advancement in technology?

4. It emphasized both capital and labor.

    What resources did neoclassical growth theory emphasize?

5. According to this theory, technology is endogenous.

    What is new growth theory?

6. He asks us to think about technology the way we think about prospecting for gold.

    How does Paul Romer ask us to think about technology?

What Is Wrong?

1. Absolute real economic growth refers to an increase in per capita GDP from one period to the next.

    Absolute real economic growth refers to an increase in Real GDP from one period to the next.

2. Economic growth can occur from below, on, or from beyond the production possibilities frontier.

    Economic growth can occur from below or on the production possibilities frontier—but not from beyond it.

3. Economic growth that occurs from an inefficient level of production shifts the LRAS curve to the right.

    Economic growth that occurs from an efficient level of production shifts the LRAS curve to the right.

4. Countries rich in natural resources will grow faster than countries poor in natural resources.

    Countries rich in natural resources will grow faster than countries poor in natural resources, ceteris paribus. Alternatively, you could write: Countries rich in natural resources will not necessarily grow faster than countries poor in natural resources.

5. According to neoclassical growth theory, technology is endogenous; according to new growth theory, technology is exogenous.

    According to neoclassical growth theory, technology is exogenous; according to new growth theory, technology is endogenous.

Multiple Choice

1. d
2. a
3. c
4. a
5. b
6. e
7. a
8. a
9. c
10. b
11. c
12. e
13. b
14. c
15. e

True-False

16. T
17. F
18. T
19. F
20. T

Fill in the Blank

21. rise
22. rise
23. Rule of 72
24. population
25. inefficient

Chapter 17
Answers

Review Questions

1. People in different countries trade with each other for the same reason that people within a country trade with each other—to make themselves better off.
2. Through specialization, countries (as a group) can end up producing more than if they don't specialize. Since they can produce more through specialization, the possibility certainly exists that they can consume more, too. This is accomplished by their trading with each other.
3. A tariff will lower consumers' surplus.
4. A quota will raise producers' surplus.
5. The benefits of the tariff may be concentrated over relatively few producers and the costs of the tariff may be dispersed over relatively many consumers. As a result, the average producer may receive more in gains than the average consumer loses, although consumers (as a group) lose more than producers (as a group) gain. This means the average producer has a sharper incentive to lobby for the tariff than the average consumer has to lobby against it.
6. Industries that are new (infants) in one country may have a hard time competing against their counterparts in other countries that have been around for awhile (and therefore are adults). The infant industries may need some assistance (protection) until they grow up and mature and are ready to compete on an equal basis.
7. A country is said to be dumping goods if it sells a good for less than its cost and below the price charged in the domestic market. Some people argue that this is unfair to domestic industries and therefore they should be protected from this action.
8. No, not necessarily. An economist might ask: What was the price to save the domestic job? If consumers have to pay $60,000 (in higher prices) to save every $40,000 job, it isn't worth saving those jobs.
9. The WTO's objective is to help trade flow "smoothly, freely, fairly, and predictably." It does this by administering trade agreements, assisting developing countries in trade-policy issues, and cooperating with other international organizations.
10. It means that the gains to the winners (or beneficiaries) of tariffs are less than the costs (or losses) to the losers.

Problems

1.

Opportunity cost of one unit of X for Country A	Opportunity cost of one unit of Y for Country A	Opportunity cost of one unit of X for Country B	Opportunity cost of one unit of Y for Country B
1.5Y	0.67X	1Y	1X

2. Area 1
3. Area 2
4. Change in consumers' surplus is the loss of areas 3, 4, 5, 6. Change in producers' surplus is the gain of area 3.
5. Gain from the tariff is area 3 (for producers) and area 5 (for government). Loss is the areas 3, 4, 5, and 6 (for consumers).
6. Net loss is the areas 4 and 6.
7. Area 5

8.

Price after quota	Loss in consumers' surplus due to the quota	Gain in producers' surplus due to the quota	Increase in revenue received by importers due to the quota	Net loss due to the quota
P_Q	Areas 3, 4, 5, 6	Area 3	Area 5	Areas 4 and 6

What Is the Question?

1. This will allow the country to consume beyond its production possibilities frontier (PPF).

    What will specialization and trade do for a country (in terms of its consumption)?

2. As a result, imports decrease.

    What will happen to imports as a tariff or quota is imposed?

3. The sale of goods abroad at a price below their cost and below the price charged in the domestic market.

    What is dumping?

4. The situation in which a country can produce a good at lower opportunity cost than another country.

    What does comparative advantage refer to?

5. The gains are less than the losses plus the tariff revenues.

    What is the net effect of a tariff?

What Is Wrong?

1. A PPF for the world can be drawn when 1) countries do not specialize and trade and 2) when they do specialize and trade. The world PPF will be the same in both cases.

    The world PPF will be further to the right when countries specialize and trade than when they do not.

2. The national-defense argument states that certain goods are necessary to the national defense and therefore should be produced only by allies.

    The national-defense argument states that certain goods are necessary to the national defense and therefore should be produced only by the domestic country.

3. A quota raises more government revenue than a tariff.

    A quota doesn't raise tariff revenue.

4. Consumers' surplus and producers' surplus fall as a result of a tariff being imposed on imported goods.

    Only consumers' surplus falls as a result of a tariff. Producers' surplus rises.

5. What producers gain from a quota is greater than what consumers lose from a quota.

    What producers gain from a quota is less than what consumers lose from a quota.

6. If the United States sells a good for less in France than it does in Brazil, then the United States is said to be dumping goods in France.

    The United States may not be dumping goods in this situation. Dumping requires the United States to sell goods for less than cost and less than the price charged in the domestic economy.

7. A voluntary export restraint is an agreement between two countries in which importing countries voluntarily agree to limit their imports of a good from another country.

    A voluntary export restraint is an agreement between two countries in which the exporting country voluntarily agrees to limit its exports of a good to another country.

8. A quota is a tax on the amount of a good that may be imported into a country.

    A tariff is a tax on the amount of a good that may be imported into a country.

Multiple Choice
  1. c
  2. a
  3. d
  4. a
  5. a
  6. c
  7. d
  8. d
  9. a
  10. e
  11. d
  12. e
  13. b
  14. d
  15. c

True-False
  16. F
  17. T
  18. T
  19. T
  20. T

Fill in the Blank
  21. antidumping
  22. fall
  23. falls
  24. less
  25. more (greater)

Chapter 18
Answers

Review Questions

1. A person in the United States wants to buy a British good. The American has to supply dollars in the foreign exchange market in order to buy pounds.
2. A German wants to buy a U.S. good. The German has to supply marks (in the foreign exchange market) in order to demand dollars.
3. The current account balance takes into account more items than the merchandise trade balance. The merchandise trade balance looks at the difference between merchandise exports and merchandise imports. The merchandise account balance takes into account exports of goods and services (one component of which is merchandise exports), imports of goods and services (one component of which is merchandise imports) and net unilateral transfers abroad.
4. Outflow of U.S. capital and inflow of foreign capital.
5. With a flexible exchange rate system, the demand for and supply of currencies determine equilibrium exchange rates. It is no different than supply and demand determining the price of corn, television sets, or houses. In this case supply and demand simply determine the price of one currency in terms of another currency. With a fixed exchange rate system, governments determine the exchange rate. Under a fixed exchange rate system, exchange rates are determined by government edict, not market forces.
6. If a person in the United States wants to buy a British good, he must pay for the British good with pounds. Thus he will have a demand for pounds. How will he get these pounds? He will have to supply dollars in order to demand pounds in order to buy the British good.
7. If a person in the UK wants to buy a U.S. good, he must pay for good with dollars. Thus he will have a demand for dollars. How will he get these dollars? He will have to supply pounds in order to demand dollars in order to buy the U.S. good.
8. The dollar has appreciated. When it takes less of currency X to buy currency Y, currency X is said to have appreciated. It took $0.0094 to buy one yen on Tuesday, and $0.0090 to buy one yen on Wednesday.
9. A difference in income growth rates (among countries), a difference in relative inflation rates (among countries), and changes in real interest rates (among countries).
10. Suppose the equilibrium exchange rate is $1 = 106 yen and the official exchange rate is $1 = 150 yen. The dollar is overvalued.
11. Devaluation is an act of government; depreciation is an act of markets.

Problems

1. − $10
2. + $4
3. + $17
4. − $1
5. $ 0
6.

If the	Then the
demand for dollars rises in the foreign exchange market	supply of pesos rises on the foreign exchange market
demand for pesos falls on the foreign exchange market	supply of dollars falls on the foreign exchange market
demand for dollars rises in the foreign exchange market	supply of pesos rises on the foreign exchange market

7.

If	Then
$1 = 106 yen	1 yen = $0.0094
$1 = 74 Kenyan shillings	1 shilling = $0.135
$1 = 1,500 Lebanese pounds	1 pound = $0.000667

8.

The exchange rate is	And the item costs	What does the item cost in dollars?
$1 = 106 yen	18,000 yen	$169.81
$1 = £0.50	£ 34	$68
$1 = 9.44 pesos	89 pesos	$9.43

9.

The exchange rate changes from	Has the dollar appreciated or depreciated?
$2 = £1 to $2.50 = £1	depreciated
109 yen = $1 to 189 yen = $1	appreciated
10 pesos = $1 to 8 pesos = $1	depreciated

10.

If ...	The dollar will (appreciate, depreciate)
the real interest rate in the U.S. rises relative to real interest rates in other countries	appreciate
income in foreign countries (that trade with the U.S.) rises relative to income in the United States	appreciate
the inflation rate in the U.S. rises and the inflation rate in all other countries falls	depreciate

11.

If the equilibrium exchange rate is $1 = £ 0.50 and the official exchange rate is	Then the dollar is (overvalued, undervalued)
$1 = £ 0.60	overvalued
$1 = £ 0.30	undervalued

What Is the Question?

1. Any transaction that supplies the country's currency in the foreign exchange market.

    What is a debit?

2. Any transaction that creates a demand for the country's currency in the foreign exchange market.

    What is a credit?

3. The summary statistic for the exports of goods and services, imports of goods and services, and net unilateral transfers abroad.

    What is the current account balance?

4. The difference between the value of merchandise exports and the value of merchandise imports.

    What is the merchandise trade balance?

5. One-way money payments.

    What are unilateral transfers?

6. The price of one currency in terms of another currency.

    What is the exchange rate?

7. It predicts that the exchange rates between any two currencies will adjust to reflect changes in the relative price levels of the two countries.

    What does the purchasing power parity theory predict?

8. Raising the official price of a currency.

    What is revaluation?

What Is Wrong?

1. The balance of payments is the summary statistic for the current account balance, capital account balance, net unilateral transfers abroad, and statistical discrepancy.

    The balance of payments is the summary statistic for the current account balance, capital account balance, official reserve balance, and statistical discrepancy.

2. The demand for dollars on the foreign exchange market is linked to the supply of dollars on the foreign exchange market. In short, if the demand for dollars rises, the supply of dollars rises, too.

    The demand for dollars on the foreign exchange market is linked to the supply of other currencies on the foreign exchange market. In short, if the demand for dollars rises, the supply of other currencies rise, too.

3. There are two countries, A and B. The income of Country B rises and the income of Country A remains constant. As a result, the currency of Country B appreciates.

    There are two countries, A and B. The income of Country B rises and the income of Country A remains constant. As a result, the currency of Country B depreciates.

4. There are two countries, C and D. The price level in Country C rises 10 percent and the inflation rate in Country D is zero percent. As a result, the demand for Country C's goods rises and the supply of its currency falls.

    There are two countries, C and D. The price level in Country C rises 10 percent and the inflation rate in Country D is zero percent. As a result, the demand for Country C's goods falls and the supply of other countries' currencies fall. Alternatively, you could write: As a result, the demand for Country C's goods falls and the demand for its currency falls.

5. A change in real interest rates across countries cannot change the exchange rate.

    A change in real interest rates across countries can change the exchange rate.

6. If the equilibrium exchange rate is £1 = $1.50, and the official exchange rate is £1 = $1.60, then the dollar is overvalued and the pound is undervalued.

    If the equilibrium exchange rate is £1 = $1.50, and the official exchange rate is £1 = $1.60, then the dollar is undervalued and the pound is overvalued.

7. A international monetary fund right is a special international money crated by the IMF.

    A special drawing right is an international money crated by the IMF.

Multiple Choice
1. c
2. a
3. c
4. b
5. c
6. a
7. e
8. c
9. a
10. a
11. b
12. d
13. d
14. b
15. a

True-False
16. T
17. F
18. T
19. F
20. T

Fill in the Blank
21. merchandise trade balance
22. purchasing power parity theory
23. fix
24. devaluation
25. fixed; flexible

Chapter 19
Answers

Review Questions

1. If the world is "becoming smaller," then what happens in other countries is "closer" to you than before, and more likely to affect you. Saying that globalization is similar to the world becoming smaller signifies that with globalization what happens in other countries is more likely than ever to affect us.

2. Examples will vary, but the example we used in the text concerned the Chinese buying U.S., thus affecting interest rates in the United States.

3. Globalization may be viewed as a world in which there are no physical, economic, or political barriers to trade. It also may be viewed the same way the 50 states are viewed within the context of the United States. Just as the residents in the 50 states can trade with each other, in a global economy, countries can easily trade with each other. Economic globalization is, in a way, similar to changing countries (of the world) into states of one country. It is similar to taking independent countries such as the United States, Russia, China, Brazil, and Japan and turning them into the United States of the World.

4. No, there have been other times when globalization was present. For example, during the mid-1880s.

5. During the Cold War, there were political barriers standing between individuals in different countries. For example, between people in the Soviet Union and people in the United States. When the Cold War ended, these barriers no longer existed, thus opening up both political and economic transactions between people in the formerly communist world and those in the capitalist world. The end-of-the Cold-War explanation of globalization today suggests that globalization would not be occurring to the degree it is if the Cold War were still going on.

6. What technological advancements can do is lower the hindrances of physical distances that act as stumbling blocks to trade. Also, computer and Internet technology makes it possible for people to communicate with others over long distances, thus increasing the probability that people will trade with each other.

7. Answers will vary, but certainly one example is a policy of either implementing tariffs or raising tariff rates.

8. Benefits of globalization include (1) increased trade and the benefits that come with trade, (2) greater income per person, (3) lower prices, (4) greater productivity and innovation.

9. The benefits are usually spread over many people while the costs are usually concentrated on certain individuals. Take a specific person, George. Some of the benefits of globalization include lower prices. One of the costs might be that George loses a job to a person living in another country. For George, his loss is very visible, while the benefits he receives from globalization (like lower prices) are relatively invisible (For example, how does he know for sure that the lower prices are due to globalization and not something else?).

10. An increase in foreign real national income can increase foreign buying of U.S. goods (i.e., it can increase U.S. exports), leading to an increase in U.S. GDP. A decrease in foreign real national income can decrease foreign buying of U.S. goods (i.e., it can decrease U.S. exports), leading to a decrease in U.S. GDP.

11. As the dollar appreciates relative to foreign currencies, a dollar fetches more units of a foreign currency, thus lowering the dollar amount that Americans have to pay for foreign goods.

12. As the dollar depreciates (relative to a foreign currency), the foreign currency appreciates. Consequently, foreign goods become more expensive for Americans and U.S. goods become cheaper for foreigners. Americans buy fewer foreign goods and foreigners buy more U.S. goods. U.S. spending on imports is likely to decline and foreign spending on (U.S.) exports is likely to rise.

13. The J-curve phenomenon relates to both a worse situation in net exports in the short run (following a depreciation in a country's currency) and later to a better situation in net exports.

14. An increase in foreign input prices will shift the U.S. SRAS curve to the left; a decrease in foreign input prices will shift the SRAS curve to the right.

15. Foreign input prices may change if (1) supply of and demand for the inputs change and (2) if the dollar appreciates or depreciates.

16. It depends on the relative shifts in the AD and SRAS curves. For example, if the AD curve changes in a different direction than the SRAS curve, and by more than the SRAS curve, then the directional

change in the AD curve will determine the overall directional change in the price level. Specifically, if the AD curve shifts right by more than the SRAS left shifts left, then the price level will rise.

17. Higher real interest rates in the U.S. will attract foreign capital to the United States, thus increasing the demand for dollars. A higher demand for dollars will lead to the dollar's appreciation (in value).

18. To finance the growing U.S. budget deficit, the U.S. Treasury will need to borrow more funds, therefore the demand for credit rises, and as it does, so does the real interest rate. In turn, the higher real interest rate draws foreign capital to the U.S., in the process increasing the demand for dollars. The higher demand for dollars leads to an appreciation in the international value of the dollar. Continuing, an appreciated dollar will make foreign goods cheaper for Americans and lead to Americans increasing their import spending.

19. Contractionary monetary policy can cause interest rates to rise, which leads to an inflow of foreign capital into the United States. The demand for dollars rises on the foreign exchange market and the dollar appreciates.

What Is the Question?

1. During a rather intense period of globalization during the 1990s and early 2000s, the unemployment rate in the U.S. was low.

   Is there any evidence that increased globalization does not cause many Americans to lose jobs?

2. Forty percent in 1946 and about 1.4 percent today.

   What was the average tariff rate in the United States in 1946 and what is it today?

3. In 1995 it was 60 times higher than it was in 1977.

   How many times higher was foreign exchange trading in 1995 than in 1977?

4. The end of the Cold War.

   According to some, what has intensified the move toward globalization in recent decades?

5. The end of the Cold War, technological changes that lower the costs of transporting goods and communicating with people, and government policy changes that express an openness toward freer markets and long distance trade.

   What are the driving forces of this most recent period of globalization?

6. Because the benefits are spread over many people and the costs are concentrated on relatively few.

   Why is it often harder to see the benefits of globalization than the costs?

7. Exports minus imports.

   What are net exports?

8. The J-curve.

   What is the curve that shows net exports getting worse in the short run after a currency depreciation but better in the long run?

9. A change in supply and demand conditions and a change in exchange rates.

Name two things that can cause foreign input prices to change?

10. This shifts the AD curve rightward and the SRAS curve leftward.

    How does dollar depreciation affect both the AD and SRAS curves?

11. There are no international feedback effects in this type of economy.

    What is a closed economy?

12. Type of fiscal policy that lowers Real GDP more in a closed economy than in an open economy.

    What is contractionary fiscal policy?

13. Type of monetary policy that lowers Real GDP more in an open economy than in a closed economy.

    What is contractionary monetary policy?

14. Type of monetary policy that raises Real GDP more in an open economy than in a closed economy.

    What is expansionary monetary policy?

15. Increases capital inflows into the country.

    How will higher real interest rates (in a country) affect capital inflows into the country?

What Is Wrong?

1. Globalization is closely aligned with a movement toward more free enterprise, restrained markets, and more freedom of government for people and goods.

    Globalization is closely aligned with a movement toward more free enterprise, freer markets, and more freedom of government for people and goods.

2. Tariff rates are higher in the United States today than they were in 1946.

    Tariff rates are lower in the United States today than they were in 1946.

3. The cost of a three-minute telephone call from New York to London was $250; in 2000, it was $10

    The cost of a three-minute telephone call from New York to London was $250; in 2000, it was 40 cents.

4. Between 1980 and 2000, income per person increased 20 percent in India.

    Between 1980 and 2000, income per person doubled in India.

5. Between 1990 and 2005, the CPI rose less fast than the import price index.

    Between 1990 and 2005, the CPI rose more quickly than the import price index.

6. Globalization causes greater income inequality.

Globalization may cause some degree of greater income inequality, but it is a point still debated among economists.

7. The benefits of globalization tend to be difficult to see, partly because they are so concentrated.

    The benefits of globalization tend to be difficult to see, partly because they are so widely dispersed.

8. Expansionary fiscal policy shifts the AD curve rightward (and under certain conditions) raises Real GDP. If the expansionary fiscal policy causes a deficit, then the government will have to borrow to finance the deficit, and interest rates will be pushed downward.

    Expansionary fiscal policy shifts the AD curve rightward (and under certain conditions) raises Real GDP. If the expansionary fiscal policy causes a deficit, then the government will have to borrow to finance the deficit, and interest rates will be pushed upward.

9. When the money supply is raised, the AD curve shifts rightward, pushing up Real GDP. Also, as a result of the increased money supply, interest rates may decline in the short run. This leads to U.S. capital inflow and an appreciated dollar.

    When the money supply is raised, the AD curve shifts rightward, pushing up Real GDP. Also, as a result of the increased money supply, interest rates may decline in the short run. This leads to U.S. capital outflow and a depreciated dollar.

10. To finance the growing budget deficit, the U.S. Treasury borrows more funds in the credit (or loanable funds) market than it would have borrowed if the latest spending had been passed.

    To finance the growing budget deficit, the U.S. Treasury borrows more funds in the credit (or loanable funds) market than it would have borrowed if the latest spending had not been passed.

11. This phenomenon in which import spending initially rises after an appreciation and then later falls is summarized in the J-curve.

    This phenomenon in which import spending initially rises after a depreciation and then later falls is summarized in the J-curve.

12. A change in the exchange rate will change the AD curve in an open economy.

    A change in the exchange rate will change both the AD and SRAS curves in an open economy.

Multiple Choice

1. b
2. b
3. e
4. d
5. d
6. b
7. c
8. d
9. a
10. c
11. a
12. e
13. b
14. d
15. e
16. b
17. d
18. c
19. a
20. b

True-False

21. T
22. T
23. F
24. T
25. F
26. T
27. T
28. F
29. T

Fill in the Blank

30. World Trade Organization
31. Policy changes
32. lower prices
33. Offshoring
34. Adam Smith
35. appreciates
36. Contractionary
37. into
38. Contractionary monetary policy
39. exchange rate

Chapter 20
Answers

Review Questions

1. When a person owns stock in a company, he or she owns a part of the assets of the company. When a person owns a bond issued by the company, the person has simply acted as a lender (of funds0 to the company. The distinction between stock owner and bond owner is that the stock owner is a part owner of the company and the bond owner is simply a lender to the company.

2. The DJIA first appeared on the scene on May 26, 1896. It was devised by Charles H. Dow. Dow took 11 stocks, summed their prices on a particular day, and then divided by 11. The "average price" was the DJIA. Dow devised the DJIA to convey some information about what was happening in the stock market (Was it rising? falling?) Today, the DJIA consists of 30 stocks (and not 11 stocks).

3. Get a loan from a bank, issue stock, issue bonds.

4. An initial public offering (IPO) is a company's first offering of stock to the public.

5. Stock is bought for the dividends it may pay and for the expected gain in price.

6. It is a fund that consists of the stocks that make up a particular index (e.g. the Standard & Poor's 500 index, the Dow Jones Industrial Average, etc.).

7. A bond can be sold for face value, less than face value, or more than face value. For example, if face value is $10,000, then a bond may fetch a price of $10,000, or, say, $9,500, or, say, $10,500.

8. Buying a bond in the primary market is buying a bond from the initial issuer of the bond (e.g., the company that issued the bond). Buying a bond in the secondary market is buying the bond from someone who previously owned the bond (and may have initially purchased it in the primary market).

9. The issuer of a bond cannot set the coupon rate of the bond at any percentage he or she wants because issuers of bonds compete with each other. If other bond issuers are issuing their bonds at a coupon rate of 10 percent, then it will be difficult for another bond issuer to issue bonds at a coupon rate of, say, 4 percent.

10. An inflation-indexed Treasury bond guarantees the purchaser a certain real rate of return while a nonindexed Treasury bond does not.

11. A buyer of a futures contract is likely to be someone who wants to protect himself from a future price change. For example, he might want to "lock in" a price at which he would buy something now, instead of waiting to later when he might have to pay a higher price for something.

12. Here is an example of how a currency futures contract work. Suppose you check the dollar price of a euro today and find that it is 83 cents. In other words, for every 83 cents, you get 1 euro in return. Let's say that you believe that in six months you will have to pay $1.10 to buy a euro. With this in mind, you enter into a futures contract: Essentially, you say that you are willing to buy $10 million worth of euros three months from now for 83 cents a euro. Who might be willing to enter into this contract with you? Anyone who thinks the dollar price of a euro will be lower (not higher) in three months. Suppose you and this other person enter a contract. You promise to buy $10 million worth of euros in three months (at 83 cents a euro) and this other person promises to sell you $10 million worth of euros in three months (at 83 cents a euro).

    Three months pass and we learn that it takes 97 cents to buy a euro (not 83 cents and not $1.10). What happens now? The person who entered into a contract with you has to buy $10 million worth of euros at an exchange rate of 97 cents = 1 euro. This means for $10 million, he gets 10,309;278 euros. He then turns these euros over to you and gets 83 cents for every euro, which gives him $8,556,701. Obviously this person has taken a loss – he spent $10 million to get $8,556,701 in return. That's a loss of $1,443,299.

    But what about you? You now have 10,309,278 euros for which you paid $8,556,701. How many dollars will you get if you sell all those euros? Well, since you get 97 cents for every euro, you will get approximately $10 million. Are you better off or worse off now? You are better off by $1,443,229.

13. Call options give the owner of the option the right to buy shares of a stock at a specified price within the time limits of the contract. The specified price at which the buyer can buy shares of a stock is called the *strike price*. For example, suppose Brown buys a call option for $20. The call option specifies that he can buy 100 shares of IBM stock at a strike price of $150 within the next month. If the price of IBM stocks falls below $150, Brown doesn't exercise his call option. He simply tears it up and accepts the fact that he has lost $20. If he still wants to buy IBM stock, he can do so through his stockbroker as he normally does and pay the going price, which is lower than $150. But if the price rises above $150, he exercises his call option. He buys the stock at $150 a share and then turns around and sells it for the higher market price. He has made a profit.

14. A PE ratio of 13 means that the stock is selling for a share price that is 13 times earning per share.

Problems

1. 20 percent
2. 26.67
3. $540
4. Take a bond with a face value of $1,000 and a coupon rate of 5 percent. Now suppose the price paid for the bond is $900. It follows that the yield is equal to the coupon payment ($50) divided by the price of bond ($900). This gives us a yield of 6 percent. In short, if the price of the bond is lower than the bond's face value, then the yield on the bond is greater than the coupon rate.
5. The annual coupon payment is $52; the new value of the bond (after inflation) is $1,034.
6. Jones has to buy $20 million worth of euros at 83 cents per euro. This turns into 24,096,386 euros. In then turns this over to Smith, receiving 77 cents per euro in return. This means he receives $18,554,217. His loss is the difference between $20 million and $18,554,217, or $1,445,783.
7. Yes. A call option gives the owner of the option to right to buy shares of a stock at a specified price during a certain time period. For example, Yvonne may have the right to buy 100 shares of stock at $150 per share. If the market price is less than $150, Yvonne will not exercise her call option, but will instead buy the shares of stock at the price less than $150. However, if market price is more than $150, Yvonne will exercise her call option and buy 100 shares of stock at a price of $150, which is less than the market price.

What Is the Question?

1. A claim on the assets of a corporation that gives the purchaser a share in the corporation.

    What is stock?

2. May 26, 1896.

    When did the Dow Jones Industrial Average first appear on the scene?

3. 30 stocks.

    How many stocks compose the DJIA?

4. The editors of the *Wall Street Journal*.

    Who decides the stocks that compose the DJIA?

5. Payments made to stockholders based on a company's profits.

    What are dividends?

6. Dividend per share divided by the closing price per share of the stock.

    What is the yield of a stock equal to?

7. The closing price per share of a stock divided by the net earnings per share.

    What is the PE ratio equal to?

8. The yield and price paid are inversely related.

    What is the relationship between the yield of a bond and the price paid for the bond?

9. Annual coupon payment divided by the price paid for the bond.

    What does the yield (or interest rate) on a bond equal?

10. First issued in 1997.

    When did the federal government first issue inflation –indexed Treasury bonds?

11. A contract in which the seller agrees to provide a particular good to the buyer on a specified future date at an agreed-upon price.

    What is a futures contract?

12. A contract that gives the owner the right, but not the obligation, to buy or sell shares of a stock at a specified price on or before a specified date.

    What is an option?

13. It will sell for a fraction of the price of the stock?

    What is a chief price characteristic of a call option?

14. A stock that plunges fast and furiously, much like an airplane that hits an air pocket.

    What is an air pocket stock?

What Is Wrong?

1. An example of a broad-based stock index is the Wilshire, which consists of the stocks of about 5,000 firms.

    An example of a broad-based stock index is the Wilshire, which consists of the stocks of about 6,500 firms.

2. The yield of a stock is equal to the dividend per share divided by the stock's PE ratio.

    The yield of a stock is equal to the dividend per share divided by the closing price per share.

3. As the price for a bond falls, the yield on the bond falls too.

    As the price for a bond falls, the yield on the bond rises.
    As the price for a bond rises, the yield on the bond falls.

4. When it comes to bonds, the number after the colon (as in 105:12) stands for 16ths of $10.

    When it comes to bonds, the number after the colon (as in 105:12) stands for 32nds of $10.

5. Call options give the owner the right, but not the obligation, to sell shares of a stock at a strike price during some period of time.

> *Call options give the owner the right to buy shares of a stock at a strike price during some period of time.*

Multiple Choice
1. b
2. a
3. a
4. b
5. b
6. c
7. b
8. c
9. e
10. d

True-False
11. F
12. F
13. T
14. T
15. T

Fill in the Blank
16. Bo Derek
17. put options
18. bond
19. PE ratio
20. opposite

Chapter 21
Answers

Review Questions

1. Demand is inelastic. If price falls and total revenue falls too, then demand must be inelastic.
2. Major changes in the weather affect the supply curve and price. Idemand is inelastic, then quantity demanded will not change much as price changes a lot. Since price and quantity demanded change in opposite directions, a large fall in price combined with a small change in quantity demanded will dramatically lower total revenue. Alternatively, a large rise in price combined with a small change in quantity demanded will dramatically raise total revenue.
3. To avoid the risk of lower prices in the future.
4. Bad weather for all farmers but Farmer Jones means price is high (for Jones) and so is his output. High price and high output mean high total revenue, at least higher total revenue than would be the case if there is good weather for all and price is low.
5. A surplus, fewer exchanges, higher prices paid by consumers, and government purchase and storage of the surplus.
6. If the target price is $6, farmers will want to supply Q_1. At this quantity, the market price is $2. The deficiency payment is $4 per unit; the total deficiency payment is $4 multiplied by Q_1.

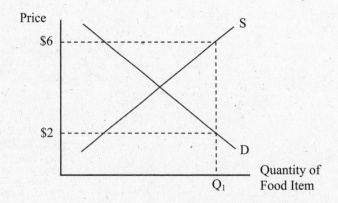

7. Production flexibility contract payments are direct payments to farmers. Let's look at an example to see how a farmer's payment is calculated. Suppose a corn farmer has 500 acres of land on which he has previously contracted to grow corn. The federal government may use, say, 85 percent of this contract acreage—or 425 acres—to calculate his payment. The 425 acres is multiplied by the yield per acre. If the yield is 105 bushels of corn per acre, the total number of bushels used in the payment calculation is 44,625 bushels. Next, the total number of bushels of corn is multiplied by a corn payment rate. This is the amount paid per unit of production to each participating farmer. Assume that the corn payment rate is $0.41 per bushel. This amount multiplied by 44,625 bushels of corn equals $18,296, which is the production flexibility contract payment for the corn farmer.
   Thus, the following equation is used to calculate a farmer's payment:

   Payment = Contract acreage x 0.85 x Yield per acre x Crop payment rate

8. A farmer pledges so many bushels of his or her crop – say 1,000 bushels. in return, the farmer receives a loan which equals the loan rate times the 1,000 bushels. The farmer can either repay the loan with interest and get back his 1,000 bushels, or simply forfeit the 1,000 bushels and keep the loan. If the market price of the crop is greater than the loan rate, the farmer will repay the loan and sell the crop at the market price. If the market price of the crop is less than the loan rate, the farmer will not repay the loan.

Problems

1.

If demand for the food item is	And supply of the food item	Then farmers' income (rises, falls, remains unchanged)
elastic	rises	rises
inelastic	rises	falls
inelastic	falls	rises

2.

Target price	Market price	Quantity supplied at target price	Deficiency payment
$4	$1	4,000 units	$12,000
$5	$5	3,000 units	$0
$6	$3	10,000 units	$30,000

3. The policy shifts the supply curve from S1 to S2 and raises the price of the food item (or crop).

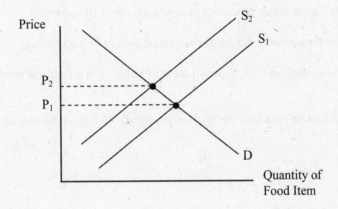

What Is the Question?

1. An obligation to make or take delivery of a specified quantity of a good at a particular time in the future at a price agreed on when the contract is signed.

   What is a futures contract?

2. A government-mandated minimum price for agricultural products.

   What is a price support?

3. It restricts output by limiting the number of farm acres that can be used to produce a particular crop.

   How does the acreage allotment program work?

4. They are similar to production flexibility contract payments and direct payments except that they are based on the difference between an effective price (established for the crop) and a target price.

   What are counter-cyclical payments?

5. It is a particular type of price support; in fact, it is the major way the government supports crop prices.

   What is a nonrecourse commodity loan?

What Is Wrong?

1. When agricultural productivity increases, the supply of food items shifts right, price falls, and total revenue (received by farmers) rises if demand is inelastic.

    When agricultural productivity increases, the supply of food items shifts right, price falls, and total revenue (received by farmers) falls if demand is inelastic. Alternatively, you coiuld write; When agricultural productivity increases, the supply of food items shifts right, price falls, and total revenue (received by farmers) rises if demand is elastic.

2. The demand for many farm products is income inelastic, which means that quantity demanded changes by a large percentage than income changes.

    The demand for many farm products is income inelastic, which means that quantity demanded changes by a smaller percentage than income changes.

3. In 2004, about 10 percent of U.S. farmers received subsidy payments.

    In 2004, about 40 percent of U.S. farmers received subsidy payments.

4. Today, one farmer in the United States produces enough food to feed 100 people.

    Today, one farmer in the United States produces enough food to feed 35 people.

5. Income elasticity of demand measures the responsiveness of a change in quantity demanded to changes in price.

    Income elasticity of demand measures the responsiveness of a change in quantity demanded to changes in income.

Multiple Choice
1. a
2. c
3. e
4. d
5. c
6. a
7. c
8. b
9. b
10. a

True-False
11. T
12. F
13. T
14. T
15. F

Fill in the Blank
16. inelastic; falls
17. Income elasticity of demand
18. price floor
19. higher prices
20. 35